JUST A LITTLE GIRL

Despair and Deliverance

by

ANNA HALBERSTAM RUBIN

AHR Books, Palo Alto, CA

This book is dedicated to my parents, my four siblings,
my aunts, my uncles, my grandmothers, and my cousins
who were all murdered
for no other reason than being Jews.

PREFACE

This work is based on my personal experience. I am a World War II survivor of one particular branch of the prominent Halberstam family: the Hasidic European dynasty founded in the eighteenth century by the eminent Judaic scholar and Hasidic leader Reb Chaim Halberstam (the Rebbe of Sanz). The appended family tree gives the exact line of descent connecting me, the young girl of the story, with the founder of the dynasty. The grandfather in the story and I were the only two members of our immediate family to make it out of Europe after the War.

Does anyone need to read another Holocaust memoir? Despite the voluminous Holocaust literature, few accounts exist of isolated individuals who survived in hiding and/or through concealing their true identity, and even fewer such are historically authentic. This case study, which took place during the years 1942-1946 adds a valuable record of one individual's journey through Hades, the horror Europe's Jews faced during the Holocaust of World War II.

Historically, the narrative is a participant observer's account: the author, narrator, and heroine are the same. I describe what I experienced. Unlike so many others who traveled similar journeys but died and cannot recount their experiences, I was fortunate enough to survive and am here to tell my tale.

As a young Jewish girl coming of age during the Holocaust, the challenges and travails I faced are potentially universal human experiences, and deserve wide readership. I hope my tale will be heard!

Although the events and episodes of the story are historical fact chronicling three years of my struggle for survival, the details supplied are not all related in the same sequence as they happened. I also omitted names and dates and supplied alternate names for some of the people involved. I have written this book 45-50 years after the facts, from memory, without the aid of notes. In spite of that, I strove for authenticity and historical accuracy in depicting the course of my struggle, its emotional impact on me, and its influence upon my development.

I was fortunate to have escaped the worst fate that befell millions of my fellow Jews- incarceration in a concentration camp and its tragic consequences- being among those very few whose efoorts to evade murderers succeeded. Why I succeeded where so many others failed remains shrouded in mystery. Perhaps a combination of factors aided me: the initiative taken by my parents who sent me away from home at a crucial time; my Orthodox upbringing which kept a degree of hope and faith alive; my youth which enabled me to view the events with a measure of curiosity and detachment; my ready adaptability to conditions at hand, and finally what some will call chance and I will call Providence — all of these may have played a role in my survival.

Whatever the reason for my survival, my mission at the end of the struggle, although postponed for half a century, became clear: I must leave a record recreating my exceptional journey through that underworld — that dark period of my life — enumerating some of the innocent people along the way who did not come back to tell their tales: among them members of my family, and friends. These people left no record behind; the world knows nothing of their existence. Yet they existed; they were flesh and blood imbued with all attributes of human beings: they had needs, hopes and aspirations; they knew of affection and chagrin, of love and hate. They dreamed of freedom and salvation often during long periods of incredible sorrow. Whether they were put to death at once, or had struggled for years, all of them had known the extremes of humiliation, hunger, pain and tortures impossible to describe, before facing inevitable, inescapable death.

Let this book, then, be a memorial to them all who suffered thus — the relatives, the friends and the strangers among them — for they held the torch to light my way while they could and they strengthened my will to survive.

FAMILY TREE

Rabbi Chaim Halberstam
(Sanz, Poland,
the Sanzer Rebbe, the "Divrei Chaim")

|

Rabbi Yechezkel Shraga Halberstam (Siniewa, Poland,
the Schiniever Rebbe, the "Divrei Yechezkel")

|

Rabbi Sholom Halberstam
(Stropkov, Slovakia, later Košice, Slovakia/Hungary,
The Alter Stropkover Rebbe, the great grandfather in the story)

|

Rabbi Menachem Mendel Halberstam of Stropkov, Slovakia
(The Stropkover Rebbe, the grandfather in the story)

|

Rabbi Yechezkel Shraga Halberstam
(Vranov nad Topľou, Slovakia, the author's father)
m. Chaya Sara (Šarlota) Rubin (Wiśnicz, Poland, the author's
mother, daughter of Rabbi Naftali Rubin, Wiśniczer Rav)

|

Anna (Chana Shaindel) Halberstam Rubin, the author
Siblings
Chaim (Heinrich),
Shmuel (Samuel),
Tzipora (Klara) and
Dovid (David) Halberstam

ACKNOWLEDGMENT

This story bears witness to the fact that in the darkest of hours, in the very centers of persecution and brutality, individuals would come forth who disregarded their personal safety and gave assistance and succor to save an isolated human being in need. Many of them were simple people moved by no elaborate ideology or philosophy. They responded automatically, almost instinctively, with simple human decency rejecting the dictum of the prevailing authority, its cruelty and its system of values.

I, the young girl in this tale, would not have survived were it not for the assistance of several such individuals who gave advice, shelter and food, and who protected me from a fate of oppression and death. To them — wherever they are — goes my personal gratitude, but also that of the entire humane community: it is because of such people — who were there at many an unexpected turn to thwart the evil design — that the best in the legacy of humane values was preserved.

So many have helped me produce this book by giving suggestions and feedback and encouragement as well as hours of their time and I wish to thank all of them. Tony Zupancic helped me present the material in this book to so many various audiences. My daughter, Dr. Haya Rubin, provided hundreds of hours of help with proofreading, editing, and converting the Word file to Kindle and print. Jerryl Lynn Rubin, Amanda Devons and Bud Rubin provided never-ending encouragement by purchasing copies of this book years in advance, motivating me to keep going on countless occasions. They also referred me to Denise Newman, who generously donated all her superb graphic design services for the cover page, and to Abby LeForge, who completed formatting the text despite it taking may more hours than she had originally agreed to work. Yaakov Jeffries took many excellent photographs of the forged identity document I used during the war, which appears on the cover, and also provided computer, software, and internet assistance on many occasions.

I thank others in my family, including my daughter, Mimi Kipper, my daughter-in-law, Yocheved Rubin, and all my grandchildren and great-grandchildren for being supportive of me and my endeavors. I thank my many other relatives, friends, and well-wishers who helped me with many other things while I worked on this book, and gave their time and energy and general encouragement, but whose names are omitted.

Finally, I thank you, my reader, for attending to my story, and for coping with the inevitable errors which I have overlooked or which I have been unable to fix.

TABLE OF CONTENTS

Preface   v

Family Tree   vii

Acknowledgment   ix

Part I: Spring 1942: Uprooting   1

    Chapter One: Sheinda   3

    Chapter Two: Another Town   12

    Chapter Three: She Is Going Home   24

    Chapter Four: Mama   35

Part II: Fall 1942: Escape   45

    Chapter Five:Deportation   47

    Chapter Six: Surviving   61

    Chapter Seven: Escape   72

Part III: Summer 1943: Survival   89

    Chapter Eight: The Metropolis   91

    Chapter Nine: The Hospital   99

Part IV: Winter 1944: Return   107

    Chapter Ten: Flight   109

    Chapter Eleven: In Shelter   125

    Chapter Twelve: Reunion   131

    Chapter Thirteen: Back In The City   155

    Chapter Fourteen: The Seamstress   170

    Chapter Fifteen: The Bunker   183

Part V: Spring 1945: Departure   193

    Chapter Sixteen: The Journey   195

    Chapter Seventeen: Freedom   198

    Chapter Eighteen: A New Life   213

Afterword   225

PART I

SPRING 1942:

UPROOTING

CHAPTER ONE
SHEINDA

It is a Sunday morning in March. A small girl with petite features and curly blond hair is walking slowly up a hilly street of this new section of her little town. Now and then she breaks her stride and looks around her.

The day promises to be beautiful: bright and sunny with signs of awakening life. The deep blue sky, the new buds on the trees, the delicate little flowers peeking out from under concealing shrubs their tiny heads bending toward the sunlight – all harbingers of spring. The morning stillness is broken only by the faint barking of a distant dog and by the chirping of flying birds. The girl takes note of it all, but is much too troubled to enjoy it.

She is aiming for the house at the top of the hill visible in the distance. The house is white, a modern structure that abruptly ends the street.

"This is it then," she reflects, "the home of the director of the high school, whom I am to confront today with that horrid request."

She is on this errand against her will, unprepared to handle what she must do and is very upset. As she walks, she recalls the scene in her home that morning: her mother insisting that she must go, she resisting and obeying only when it becomes clear to her that there is no way out.

The school director is a man Sheinda has been avoiding for as long as she can remember. It all goes back to the time when her parents had withdrawn her from the local public school, an act that caused her much embarrassment and chagrin. She was too young, only ten years old then, and didn't understand the consequences of that event. All she knew was that she missed school, her friends, her teachers, and the activities connected with them ever since. School had been important to her and life without it became vexing and confusing. Now she is on her way to do what? Solicit the good will of a person she was avoiding for so long? Ask for his intervention, his assistance? Yes, but she senses that it is so wrong; he is not the man to help her. On the contrary: he must be aware, he must long since have perceived the reality behind her special situation.

As she is nearing the house, her apprehension takes on physical symptoms — weakness in the knees and a sinking in the pit of her stomach. She summons up whatever energy she has to steady herself. She raises her hand and presses the bell. All she wants now is to get it over with as quickly as possible. She hears the sudden shrill ring of the bell as it rends the morning stillness; listens to its reverberations with a pounding heart and waits, expecting to hear footsteps. There is no response. Reluctantly she presses the bell again, and waits with a growing sense of foreboding.

Suddenly she hears someone. The door opens revealing a middle-aged woman wrapped in a pink robe.

"What is it you want?" she asks, angrily thrusting her face forward, "Don't you know better than to disturb people on a Sunday morning?"

"I -- err -- I must speak to his Excellency the director," Sheinda murmurs this in a barely audible voice shaking with fright, "Please, I will only take a few minutes," she pleads while choking on the tears she can no longer hold back. The tears suddenly released flow freely, flooding her face and highlighting her contorted features. The woman is taken aback as if moved by the sudden spectacle.

"All right, then," she says, "but I don't answer for what happens getting him out of bed for you." She closes the door and disappears into the interior, leaving the girl standing outside.

The girl is shaken but at the same time relieved. She knows the worst is yet to come. "But at least I was able to get this far" she reflects, "I got my foot in the door, didn't I"? She wipes away her tears, trying to compose herself, and resumes her waiting.

After an interval of about twenty minutes, the director opens the door. He, too, is clad in a robe over his pajamas and is fumbling with the belt trying to fasten it. He is a rather short man with stocky build. His thin brown hair is slicked back toward the center of his balding head. His steely blue eyes are clear and alert, accustomed to take in all. He is obviously making an effort to control his anger at being so unexpectedly roused.

"Yes? What do you want?" He asks gruffly, looking intently, with some surprise, at his unlikely visitor.

"I have come to ask a great favor of you," The words spill from her mouth; she appears unaware of what she is saying. The entire proceeding has taken on a dreamlike aspect for her. She hears herself continue:

"I need a statement from you — testimony to the authorities — that you are aware of my illness. If they know I am ill, they might spare me; allow me to remain at home with my family. Otherwise I will be sent away. You have heard of the decree concerning young Jewish people, haven't you? Won't you, please, give me some statement that might help me?"

As he stands listening to her, the director grows visibly angry. His face begins changing color turning crimson at last. His eyes bulge, flashing fire. Suddenly he turns on her shouting:

"So that's who you are! The ex-student whose family perpetrated the famous swindle; who cheated the state and the school system by pretending that you are too ill to go to school. And you collaborated with them! What a shame! What an outrage! Don't you people realize that we know the truth? You have been violating the law by claiming a falsehood! You are not ill! You are no more ill than I am! All these lies, and for what? What purpose did they serve? To relieve you of your civic duty — and privilege — of attending school; of getting a decent education? Now you have the audacity to come to me! You are asking me to become a party to your cheating and to your lies!"

Frightened by the ferocity of the sudden onslaught, little Sheinda breaks down and weeps. The humiliating charge against her shakes her to the core. The worst part about the accusations is her awareness that they contain a kernel of truth. "Yes", she thought to herself, "I have been involved — even if reluctantly — in schemes by my parents to remove me from school. Had I been older, I might have resisted. I might have found some way to continue my education. As it was, I just stood by and did nothing."

She remembers that event in all its detail. How she struggled against meddling by her parents. Yes, they had forbidden her participation in the Sokol. The Sokol, forbidden to her! How could they expect her to obey? The Sokol was the forum where schoolwork ended and special fun began. It was the place where twice every week after school hours her group would gather. Led by the teacher who had been her instructor through fifth grade and whom she worshiped, they would go through the routines of rhythmic dancing, singing and gymnastics. These activities exhilarated her and nurtured her civic consciousness and pride.

How torn she had been by the conflict to remain a student in good standing as well as an obedient daughter. How she struggled against having to make a choice. In the end the necessities of school had won out. She began attending the Sokol secretly, without the knowledge of her parents, inventing the excuse of additional choir practice. She was able to evade them for a while, only to be confronted by her mother who one day unexpectedly appeared at the Sokol and dragged her crying out of the gym. The episode had been shattering and the Sokol became a memory and a longing....

There had also been the time of her participation in the school play. Sheinda had been chosen for a special part and was to wear a kroy, the national costume. She conspired with a neighbor, a seamstress, who was to create the outfit. Her teacher, suspecting that she had no support at home, assisted in her preparations. She managed to carry it off, but with diminished enjoyment, on account of having to conceal the project from her parents.

So it went with other activities. There was no question of her taking part in the Slovenska Beseda, the school dance that took place at the end of the school year. When asked by her teacher if she will be able to participate, her desire to do so got the better of her judgment. She told the teacher: "Yes, I will." She carried on with the pretense long enough to be assigned a dancing partner, while she knew all along that her participation would be vicarious — confined to watching from the stands. And so it was.

How religiously she stood there outside the schoolyard fence looking in. She watched her classmates swirling gaily to the music — the bright-multicolored layered petticoats of the girls rising and falling with the rhythm of the songs. The boys, festive in their colorful trousers shirts and vests led them through the well-known steps of the various dances. How exhilarating it seemed, how she longed to be part of it....

6

What Sheinda desired mainly was to be one of the gang — to be able to follow the routine without special attention from others, as was too often the case. "Why am I the only one not attending school on Saturdays?" she wondered rebelliously. Although the other Jewish students had been excused from work they couldn't perform on the Sabbath, their presence was required and they were there. "I alone must always be absent," she often thought with resentment. She recalls one such episode.

She can see the room with all the girls in it. Her seat is the second one in the first row on the right side of the room. A few steps away there is a large platform with the teacher's desk and behind it hangs the large blackboard. The teacher, a pretty dark haired woman in her thirties, neatly dressed, sits in her chair behind the desk preparing the next activity for her class. The girls are finishing their compositions, carefully writing each sentence in the special notebooks kept in school. This is the work the teacher will grade, so they pay special attention. Now it is time to take a break from their work. It is time for them to relax, lean back in their seats and listen as the teacher reads, opening new worlds of adventure and mystery. This time she is reading from Malý Lordik (Little Lord Fauntleroy). The story is good, fascinating — from a world so different from their own. She listens in great concentration, imagining herself to be there in that far away land, oblivious to her own surroundings. Suddenly, she hears a jarring sound: "Anča (her secular name), it's time for you to go."

She reels back to reality. The voice is the teacher's who has just announced that she must leave now. It has started...her special torment. Not only will she miss the fun of the rest of this activity; She must now step into the hated role of being singled out...of being different.

She quickly puts her belongings into her school bag and makes her way as quietly as she can manage to the wall on her right, along which are the cubbyholes with hooks for their outdoor clothes. Her back is turned to the class as she reaches for her coat and hat and she is glad not to have to face them; she knows that all eyes are on her back. She manages to keep her composure while she dresses, but she knows that she lacks the poise to say good-bye gracefully. She takes the first few steps toward the door at the other end of the room, she mumbles good-bye and quickly runs out of the room. Nor is this the end of the story: She will have to go through this same thing next week, and the week after and on every Friday for the rest of the winter season!

When her parents had finally decided to withdraw her from school, Sheinda had become tired of the struggle; of having to put up a fight for what other students could simply take for granted. So she stood by helplessly, allowing their scheme to succeed. She sensed however that her family had acted out of noble rather than base motives. Deeply pious people, they wished to shield her: protect her from the "harmful" influences of secular study and life. They were convinced that they acted with her best interests at heart. And so they had. For, in truth — except for the means they had sometimes employed — their action was totally consistent with their value system and their way of life. They could be faulted neither in principle nor in logic.

But how is she to convey all of that to this man who now stands before her boiling with righteous indignation? How is she to impart to him her own helplessness over the decision her family had taken and the suffering it had caused her? She cannot! These are truths she can barely perceive: She feels it rather than knows it but is incapable of articulating any of it. She just stands there in mute isolation weeping silently.

Ach, which one of her sorrows is she bemoaning so? Is it the loss of her purposeful schooldays? Is it the rigidity of her family? Is it this grievous and futile confrontation with the director and the embarrassment it causes her? Or is it her vague perception of the sudden end of her protected childhood and the terror of the approaching menace?

She couldn't single out or point to any one of them; nor could she think of them in a concrete manner. — She cannot think at all, she can only feel. And what she feels is that her heart is breaking. It is as though all of the tribulations of her young life had come together in this sudden outpouring of grief.

The director is addressing her, interrupting her reverie:

"I cannot help you," he says abruptly. I cannot give you what you want." He turns away from her, then suddenly returns and adds as if in afterthought: "It would do you no good, anyway.

I know, believe me...I cannot help you, no one can...!" She feels herself dismissed and turns away in sorrow.

The ordeal is over and Sheinda is on her way home. She feels relief at the sudden termination of the apprehension — the dreadful spell she had been under all morning — but her sense of relief is short lived. She hasn't forgotten the reality awaiting her at home. The urgency of her errand had pushed the terrifying dilemma to the back of her consciousness; now the thought of it is coming to the fore assailing her with all its force....

She cannot recall most subsequent details of that fateful day. She doesn't remember such things as getting dressed for the journey, eating, or packing her belongings. Only isolated items stand out clearly in her memory — and these she remembers in vivid detail. She remembers the sense of urgency that surrounded her final preparations: Her broken, depressed mood — a result of both the morning errand, and her impending departure. How she took leave of her father... who embraced her warmly and placed a hurried kiss on her lips. She remembers the rush to the bus stop accompanied by her mother who helped carry her small valise.

She remembers....

The bus is late and there is a long wait in the street. Her mother uses the time to give last minute instructions.

The girl looks around and takes in all of the familiar sights: the storefront next to the bus terminal crowded with teenagers, the school building visible at the corner; the office of Dr. Engel, the town physician, with his shingle in the window. There are trees in front of the buildings and townsfolk walking by engaged in their mundane pursuits. She can see the shops across the street and some of the people who work there. Soon they will be closing up for the night to return to their homes.

How dreadful to have to leave behind so suddenly all that is familiar; all that has been part of home and all of it suddenly so irrelevant to what she is about to do....

It isn't the first time Sheinda is leaving home. When her parents had gone away occasionally during the summer months, taking only the youngest child with them, she and her siblings would be parceled out to relatives in nearby communities. She would stay with grandparents, uncles and aunts, and cousins.

9

Although she had missed home during these periodic dislocations, being away had had its compensations.

But this now is different, she reflects. "Where am I going? What will I find when I get there? How will I survive alone and what will happen to them while I am gone? When will I return…?"

She is so afraid to go, to be away from loved ones at such a threatening time when all that has been certain in life is suddenly gone; when the world as she has known it is being shattered! Isn't this the time to be near family and friends; to have their proximity, their counsel and consolation? But no, she must go…she is being sent to a place where no record of her — to trace her whereabouts — is available. It is her only chance to escape the dreaded authorities.

When the time comes to board, her mother helps the girl up and finds her a window-seat in the middle of the bus.

"Sheinda, stop crying," says her mother, trying to compose her. Sheinda has been crying all the way to the station and looks very sad. Suddenly her mother stops in her tracks. She has forgotten to bring along the sandwiches she had prepared for the journey! Will there be time to bring them before the bus leaves…? She hesitates, unable to make up her mind. She knows there is little time, but how can she let her daughter go without food? She decides to take the chance and leaves, assuring the girl of her immediate return. Soon thereafter, the driver and his assistant begin final preparations for departure. They accommodate a few latecomers; find them seats and place their luggage in the hold of the bus. The driver takes his place at the wheel while his assistant moves from passenger to passenger checking their tickets.

Sheinda sits in silence, anxiously awaiting her mother's return. She keeps looking out of the window, craning her neck in the direction whence her mother is to appear. But she doesn't see her. No, her mother is nowhere in sight.

At last all seems ready. She hears the familiar roar of the engine as the driver starts and begins moving the vehicle out into the road. He accelerates, increasing power gradually, and soon the bus is rolling along Main Street on the way out of town. Sheinda doesn't take her gaze off the window.

As the bus is passing the street leading in the direction of her home, she glimpses the figure of a woman turning the corner running toward them. The woman carries a small parcel in her right hand waving it frantically trying to stop the bus, but to no avail! The bus keeps moving on....

For a fleeting moment Sheinda is able to hold in view the image of the frantic woman desperately trying to stop the bus then, realizing the futility of it, giving up in resignation.

It is the last time she sees her mother.

CHAPTER TWO
ANOTHER TOWN

Sheinda doesn't recall much of that journey, only the stop in the little town midway to her destination, where she changes buses. Her parents had arranged a visit with a family of distant cousins, people who were total strangers to her, whom she had never seen before. Nevertheless, the Blums were decent. They waited for her at the station, which was only a short distance from their home, with their daughter, a rather tall girl of about fifteen, who was a very friendly sort. They invited her to their home, treated her to lunch and imparted whatever comfort they could. Their daughter remained with her, keeping her company until it was time for her to depart. Of the last leg of her trip, that took her to her destination, Sheinda remembers not a thing.

Her memory opens upon a scene in Perele's kitchen, a busy thoroughfare, connecting the front hall with the rest of the rooms in the dwelling, where most of the action of the household is concentrated. Perele is the rebetzin, the local rabbi's wife.

The rabbi, Reb Moishe Leib, known as the Rov, is the girl's distant relative. He is a youngish man, not very tall, but his thin frame and agility give him the appearance of height. He has a black beard and dangling curly payot (side curls). He wears the dark shiny coat and round black hat, the garb of the Hasidic rabbi. On his feet he has black loafer-like shoes above which white knee-high stockings and checkered breeches are visible.

The members of Reb Moishe Leib's community hold him in high esteem. It is common knowledge that he is a considerable talmid chochom (Torah scholar) who has been leading the community for some years. He inherited his post from his father-in-law, the eminent Hasidic leader of that town and its environs, who had served both as rebbe to his Hasidim and as chief rabbi of the town. Reb Feivele, of blessed memory, as the latter is often referred to, had selected him, Moishe Leib, from among many aspirants, and had given him his only daughter, Perele, in marriage.

Perele is a short skinny young woman with large luminous eyes. She is clad in a faded cotton dress of nondescript color and pattern, covered by a large apron. On her head she wears a simple cotton kerchief. She darts about energetically amidst her flock of children of various ages dishing out whatever is needed: exhortation, advice or reproof here; a kiss or a slap there, as the case may require, but her essential cheerfulness remains — it is always there. It is evident that she is in control, commanding obedience from all including her husband Reb Moishe Leib who time and again can be seen in the kitchen discreetly seeking her view on some pressing matter.

After arriving at the house of her relatives, Sheinda is welcomed and is assigned a place to sleep. That place is on the upper tier of a bunk in one of the small bedrooms with three of the oldest girls of the household. The oldest, a chubby outgoing youngster with thick black braids accepts her readily and her siblings follow suit. The bunk is crowded and she tosses about endlessly before she manages to sleep. The house is so noisy; there is a good deal more clatter and less order here than she is accustomed to. Still, after a while, she manages to get some rest at night and is able to settle down into her new routines. She finds the accessibility of the adults and the companionship of the children in this household rather congenial. Indeed, under normal circumstances she can envision a very pleasant time here.

It isn't very long, however, before her newly found composure disappears. People begin coming to the rabbi's house seeking his counsel. That fact in itself is nothing new. Reb Moishe Leib is used to being consulted. What is taking place now though is different. Instead of the occasional supplicant, scores of people are now coming through his doors and they keep coming during all hours, even at night. Their problems, too, are of a different sort. They are seeking advice now on matters for which he has no precedent; nothing he can fall back upon. He has been able to deal with their day-to-day exigencies — even those of late requiring sacrifice of wealth and personal possessions. The punitive legislation that stripped away their legal protection, invited violence, deprived them of a minimum sense of security had been difficult enough.

But their questions now concern life and death, their very survival. For example: should they stay put — awaiting the execution of the evil decree of deportation — or should they run for their lives? If so, where should they run? Should they go singly with every individual fending for himself, seeking his own survival, or should they cling to their families, their loved ones? And what is to become of their old and their ill, their little children? How should they defend themselves against the violence? — Insults, plunder, beatings and even killings are becoming rampant and they are unable to find recourse against them. What should they do? Reb Moishe Leib listens, but is unable to provide answers to these bewildering questions.

The town falls into the grip of a terrible panic. Mothers, fathers, town leaders — all are running about, wringing their hands and weeping helplessly! Their lament is loud, open and without consolation. Is this possible? She isn't dreaming? For the first time in her life Sheinda witnesses adults weeping when there is no funeral or some similar calamity. She watches them as they rush about, finally bringing their heartbreak to the rabbi's door.

There is a woman on the threshold of that door crying bitterly:

"What are we to do, Rebbe, tell us; show us what to do! They are throwing us out of the only home we have ever known, our sole livelihood, with nothing but a bundle on our backs. Bitter, Rebbe, bitter! Where are they taking us? Oy, Rebbe, help me! Help us, Rebenyu...!"

Another woman is sobbing, prostrate with grief:

"Help! Rebbe, help! My daughter, my only child, is gone. The police have just taken her from me. She refused to go and they dragged her, beating her mercilessly. How am I to survive; oy, how can I live without my Taibele?"

The laments are accompanied by fountains of burning tears streaming down the faces of the helpless creatures. Nor are they alone, there are scores like them. Men and women everywhere stand around in small groups or in pairs weeping silently, not knowing what to do. The scene is indeed like those the young girl has come to associate with funerals, only this time the tragedy is not confined to any one single family.

The rabbi is bewildered. He has no practical advice to offer his congregants nor, for that matter, members of his own household. He cannot resolve their terrifying dilemmas. What can he do? He wants to ease their pain and resolves to maintain his composure and dignity. He goes about his tasks of teaching, study and prayer with quiet deliberation so that amidst all of the turmoil he remains an island of peace. His prayers have acquired an unusual intensity of late; they are more fervent than ever before. Sheinda can see him pacing his study, lost in thought, as though he were holding counsel with himself:

"What can I do for my poor people in their desperate situation? What is to be my role? Obviously, I can offer no satisfactory solutions to their tragic choices, but I must offer them some inspiration, some indication that I continue to keep faith with the Almighty!"

And this he does with great determination! He remains accessible to those who seek him out, encouraging their prayer, hope and faith.

Sheinda is much affected by the events around her. She writes home regularly and receives communication from them. Her parents have been keeping her abreast of developments at home. Most of the youth of their town are no longer there, they write; they have been shipped to labor camps. The rest of the community has been put on notice that they, too, will soon have to go! Her absence from home has not been a problem — thank God! They are grateful that she is within reach, that they know where she is and can write to her.

There comes the day when she is forced to separate from the rabbi's family. It comes to pass late one afternoon. Perele and her children are assembled in the kitchen. The rabbi, Reb Moishe Leib, is standing off to one side, holding on to his prayer book. He looks around the room slowly, letting his gaze linger awhile on each of his children, then on his wife.

Perele has been busy for days, trying to put together the very few essentials they are allowed to carry with them. She prepared a small bag for each member of her family — stuffing a few extra items of apparel for the little ones into her own bag. The bundles are now standing lined up against the wall. Perele looks around anxiously, then runs into an adjoining room. She returns with a handful of additional things and distributes them among the various bundles.

"R'bono shel oilom [Almighty God], what are they doing to us?" these few simple words escape her lips now, as they have done now and again during this entire process of grim, silent preparation. Only the tears, flowing profusely down her cheeks, testify to the breaking of her remarkable spirit.

The rabbi approaches her and motions to the children to come closer. When they are all together, the children in a semicircle around their parents, the rabbi says:

"They will soon be coming to take us from here, from our home. I know you are all sad: you would all rather stay here, together, and so would I. But the Almighty evidently has other plans for us. We will stay together for as long as we can, but remember, wherever you are, that everything is in the hands of the Almighty. Let him guide you in all you have to do. No matter how bad things seem to be for you, remember, Hashem is with you."

That done, Reb Moishe Leib puts his hands on the head of each child in turn and utters a silent blessing. He approaches his wife and looks at her for a moment. He sees her tear-stained face and utters a few words of comfort, then asks her forgiveness for any transgression, any grief he may have caused her. She cries and does likewise.

Sheinda stands in Perele's kitchen by the door and observes this entire scene. Her thoughts transport her to her own home....

It is Yom Kippur Eve...she sees the small room in which they dine. Everything has been washed and polished. The table is covered with their best white linen cloth; the white candles, in their silver candlesticks, are ablaze, Mama just having lit them. They have concluded their meal, the table has been cleared, the dishes piled into the kitchen. Her father, wearing a long white kittel, the garment used by Orthodox Jewish males for ceremonial purposes such as marriage, the Passover Seder, prayers on Yom Kippur and as a shroud, blesses each child. He then turns to her mother and crying audibly, asks her forgiveness. His humility causes Mama and the children to cry as well until the house resonates with weeping. Their mood is somber, but they are strangely relieved.

She hears knocking on the door, which becomes very loud. The sudden jolt brings her back to the present. One of the girls, the oldest, with the braids, opens the door. In rush members of the Garda with their weapons and clubs. They sweep through the house like a hurricane, opening doors and cupboards everywhere as if looking for someone. The roar they stir up is deafening and their hate elicits a paralyzing fear. Finally, their leader comes to a halt in front of the assembled family and motions to his men to cease their clatter. He then brings out a list on which the names of all family members are listed.

"This is the family Landes, isn't it?" he barks, then, without waiting for confirmation, proceeds to shout his instructions.

"I will read your names from this list. Each one of you must move over to where I point as soon as I have read the name! You will stand there until I've read all the names on the list, then you will follow me quietly, otherwise those dogs — you have seen them haven't you? They are waiting outside; they will deal with you! Do you understand?"

Sheinda hears all this from her concealed spot behind the kitchen door where she has been standing, with her head and shoulders pressed against the wall, ever since the police arrived. Her heart is pounding wildly and her legs tremble. The door has been left ajar as they came in; rushing through, and she pulled it against her. But what if they close it on the way out and discover her presence? What will happen to her then? She decides not to think about that possibility; to concentrate instead on controlling her fear and emotions. She cannot afford to weep, sigh, cough, or sneeze. Even her breathing must be inaudible. She will simply have to remain here, taking action a step at a time, as need arises.

The official, in the meantime, has gone through the list. The members of the rabbi's household are lined up near their packages by the wall on the other side of the open door. They are waiting for the order to pick up their bags and move, which comes presently. The members of the Garda now move out and wait in the vestibule outside the kitchen for everyone to pass through, counting the heads as each family member goes by.

Even the little ones — the youngest a boy of only five — move through the line as ordered. They obey all instructions with a serious, sad mien, sensing the tragic nature of the situation. The last one to leave the kitchen is Perele. She lingers awhile, takes one last backward glance into the kitchen and leaves, making certain that the door remains open.

The girl remains behind the door, listening attentively: she hears the front door clang shut and soon thereafter the noise of departing vehicles. She remains where she is; she knows that she must not make a move until the cover of darkness. She relaxes a bit and is immediately assailed by guilt:

"I may have escaped for a while, yes, but what about them?" She allows herself the relief of a few silent tears as she recalls the scenes she has just witnessed: the last communion of the family in their home; the incredible faith of the rabbi, the intelligent behavior of the children, and Perele's vigilance and presence of mind. Wasn't it like her to take that last, deliberate move with the door, playing them a trick, as it were; retaining her sense of humor in the face of their brutality.

Sheinda sits on the floor behind the door with her back pressed against the wall and her knees against her chin. She decides to stretch her legs and does so, thereby pushing the door slightly, but imperceptibly, away from her. This feels better. She knows she must remain sitting here for a very long time. She must try to relax, find the most comfortable position she can manage and bring her emotions and thoughts under control. She will have to decide what to do next, but not yet, no! She will just sit here quietly, letting the sudden stillness of the house calm her.

It was well after midnight when she knocked at the door of the Mueller's, her other relatives in this town with a daughter her age. Mr. Mueller, not having as yet retired for the night, heard her right away and opened the door.

He was a man of middle height with a round, cheerful face and short red beard. Generally good humored, with a twinkle in his eye, he was a raconteur with an anecdote or joke for every occasion. He liked children and they enjoyed being around him.

His wife, an attractive lady with a blond wig, was already asleep, as were the rest of the family: a son and three daughters. Like her husband, Mrs. Mueller was pleasant, outgoing and articulate. There was a good deal of lively chatter between the two of them, and between them and whoever else happened to be present.

The son, a young lad of about eighteen, was well-built, blond, with a charming face and blue eyes. Of his three sisters one was older, the other two younger than he. The youngest girl, who resembled her brother, was only about five years old. She had long flaxen curls and a sweet smile.

The sister next to her in age, Bruchi, was approaching her middle teens. She was pretty: with short fair hair, good eyes and a friendly disposition. She it was whom the young girl sought out as often as she could. Bruchi's older sister Gita, a girl of about twenty, was short, brown haired and good-natured, resembling her father in disposition. She was accomplished, with developing literary talents and a fine sense of humor.

Sheinda, exhausted and quite out of breath from her ordeal, moved through the door Mr. Mueller held open for her and sat down quietly to rest. She was relieved to be here at last, having had to run the last part of the way, impelled by her fear. After a while she told him about the events that brought her here: how they had taken away the rabbi and his family, how she remained hidden behind the door, how she waited alone till after dark, immobilized, trembling with fear. Mr. Mueller listened with gravity to all she described, puncturing her narrative with an occasional question or two. The final thing he wanted to know was whether anyone saw her coming here; did she meet anyone on the way here? Reassured that no one saw her, he fixed her something to eat and watched her wolf it down. She was very hungry now; she hadn't eaten a thing all day, but hadn't felt it at all — not until now.

As soon as she was through eating, Mr. Mueller took her to a little room that appeared to be his office. Here he improvised a bed for her, bid her good night, and departed. She fell asleep almost immediately and slept through the rest of the night.

She liked this family: they were an easygoing jolly group who even in these somber days exuded a measure of cheer. They provided the girl with much needed distraction. But in matters concerning the burning questions of the day, the impending deportation of the community and what to do about it, they couldn't be of much help; their own situation was rather shaky: their vinimka [letter of exception from deportation] wasn't foolproof and it occurred to the young girl that it isn't in her best interest to remain here. That fact was brought home to her one day soon after she arrived when the police came checking up on them. They arrived suddenly, without notice and wanted to know the identity of each family member. There had been no time for the girl to hide. She was present during the entire process, simply remaining in the background when Bruchi had been called upon to step forward. By some unexplained miracle, they didn't realize that an additional girl was present in the room. To the girl it became clear however that she isn't safe here. No, she would have to find another place, somewhere with less exposure. Her relatives agreed and began looking about for her. In the meantime, she enjoyed the comfort and companionship they provided.

She is to take leave of Bruchi and her family soon; they succeeded in finding her a place to stay. What they will do, she doesn't know. They didn't say; it's safer that way.

The people she is now staying with are an impoverished family with a house full of children presided over by a remarkable man. She doesn't know what the man does for a living, but she can see him coming and going with a smile on his face and a few cheerful words to his children and to her. There aren't any creature comforts to speak of in their place; there certainly is no abundance of food. But she feels at home and welcome to whatever they have and he manages to bring sunshine in his wake whatever the weather!

One day, a dreadful one for her, her newly found benefactor doesn't come home, he disappears. For a while no one knows where he is, what has happened to him. They imagine the worst. Eventually they hear that he is in prison. No one knows why; they aren't told why. All she knows is that he is no longer there; no longer able to provide for his family, no longer able to spread his cheer. What will happen to him? Will they ever see him again? Or is he about to become one in the growing list of victims whose whereabouts no one can account for; whose fate nobody knows? They are there one day, and are gone forever the next! She is reminded of Mr. K....

He is a tall, thin figure of dark complexion and severe manner. He was a kind man, but stern with his children, brooking no nonsense from them. They were neighbors. She frequented their house and witnessed his discipline. She feared and avoided him.

There were several beautiful girls in the household. Some still in school, others in local positions of responsibility. In the presence of Mr. K there was silence and order. They all had their chores; were expected to assist their mother, a mild-mannered individual, with her housework and their father in the store. They carried out their tasks with competence. As soon as their father was out of the way, the spirits rose. There was gaiety, laughter, singing and games of all sorts. She could count on an afternoon or evening of fun when in their presence.

The family also had two sons. The elder, a grown man when he returned home, had been away for some years. She viewed him as a stranger and avoided him. The younger, Rudy, was a growing boy rather tall for his age with pimples covering much of his face. Thin, gangly and shy, he was awkward and funny looking.

She feared some of the boys in her courtyard. They were loud, mischievous and inconsiderate. They often teased and made fun of her. They would call her "shorty" whenever they saw her passing by and would chase her, causing her to trip and fall. She was mortified at their torment. Often she would stand in some place for long periods of time — sometimes it seemed like hours — hiding, waiting to slip by unnoticed rather than venture into full view.

But Rudy was different. He never ridiculed or teased and when he found out about the others, tried to protect her. He would accompany her on errands, helped carry her bags, stood up for her. She grew to like him; to rely on him. He became the older brother she never had.

One day she was sitting on a bench in their kitchen. Rudy came in and sat down next to her. For a while they just sat there quietly without speaking. When she looked up, she noticed Rudy gazing at her with something akin to a plea in his eyes. She was puzzled, was about to speak, when he took hold of her hand and began to stroke
it gently. He moved closer, put one arm around her waist while his free hand continued to caress hers. She looked at him questioningly trying to understand....Wasn't this the game adults were playing? Will he now push her down on her back and climb on top of her...the way their maid Manya and her friend were doing? But Rudy just sat there holding her gently; he didn't say a word, just looked at her as if imploring. She didn't dislike his nearness...or the warm strange sensation of his embrace. And he seemed to be asking for discretion...!

21

Well, this was Rudy, after all. She trusted him; she knew he would never hurt her!

Toward the end of one fall day, early in October, she had accompanied Rudy and his sisters to the hub of Main Street, where a large throng of people had gathered. They were witnessing an unusual sight. Crossing the town were endless columns of soldiers on their way to the local military barracks where they were to break their journey and rest.

Soldiers in training marching through town were nothing new; they had been around for years stationed at the edge of town; indeed, they were a familiar sight. But these were not their soldiers; these were foreign troops, Germans, the dreaded enemy on their way to Russia! She stood on tiptoe on a raised hastily improvised platform and watched, spellbound, as they were moving by.

The neat columns were moving efficiently, four abreast, driven by zeal and held in thrall by their strict military discipline. Were it not for their different uniforms and language, they could easily have been mistaken for the battalions of the well-trained national army of their their former beloved republic. There was one other important difference: the sporadic violence to which these strangers were given.

On the last day of their stay in town, late at night, one of the soldiers approached the courtyard into which (earlier that day) he had seen a bearded Jew disappear. The soldier may have wanted a picture of the man; a relic of those people they were about to annihilate? The Jew, uncertain of what the soldier wanted and frightened, had given him the slip. The soldier, trying to locate him now, stopped and knocked at the door where he thought he had seen his man enter. Mr. K., whose abode was next door, heard the loud rapping: he opened his window slightly and looked out. Seeing the German, he panicked: aware that his daughters occupied the apartment nearby. He stuck his head out of the window and yelled: "Help, help, fire!" The soldier, angered at the commotion, approached the window out of which Mr. K. was leaning. He grabbed his gun and shot Mr. K. through the head, in the manner in which one swats away an annoying insect. Mr. K. died on the spot. The next morning, in the company of friends and neighbors who had gathered in their house, Sheinda saw him still lying there in a pool of blood. She would never forget the sight....

Sheinda remained with her new family for a while, for they were willing to provide her with shelter even though their breadwinner was no longer there. Then one day it dawned on her that things here are coming to an end. The community was being decimated. Every day several families were taken from their homes and soon everyone would have to go. What is she waiting for? Indeed, what is she doing here — a small girl, all alone in this strange town — at such an ominous time? She can see the logic of her having had to leave home at the time she did. That had been necessary to gain time and to delay tragedy. But what about now, when it is no longer a question of young people, when entire families are being threatened? Does it still make sense for her to remain here?

She decides that it does not. No! She isn't going to sit around and wait here any longer! She has no clearly formulated plan. All she knows is that she cannot possibly bear to witness more of what she knows is coming without the proximity of her loved ones. She decides to return home, come what may, and she advises her family of her decision. As soon as she does so, she experiences a tremendous sense of relief; as though a terrible burden has fallen off her shoulders — and she instinctively perceives that she is doing the right thing

CHAPTER THREE
SHE IS GOING HOME

Sheinda entered the narrow yard that began sloping downhill steeply a few meters from the gate. The house stood to her right — a narrow, long structure built into and sloping downward with the curves of the hill — its various apartments extending to the very bottom of the yard. She climbed the high stoop and made her way through the massive front door into the vestibule — a small square area with a door in every wall. The door to her left took her through the kitchen to the dining room, the center of the large apartment occupied by her grandparents. It was a large room with a tall ceiling and high windows. She looked across the room. Toward the end of the wall, near the windows, was a door leading out to a terrace, a large balcony with a wrought-iron railing. The balcony hung above a ravine that fell away steeply from that side of the house. At the very bottom of the ravine a shallow creek wound its way from the town's hilly part — the elevation on which the house stood — to the flats or bottom section of the town. The view from the balcony across the length of the steep ravine to the very end of the creek was intimidating — but the wide expanse of the outdoors with its abundance of color from trees, shrubs, flowers and birds lent this room substance and charm. In the center of the room stood a large table with chairs where the family took their meals and around which they were now assembled.

The grandfather sits in his chair at the head of the table. He is a short, thin figure with a longish gray beard that divides into several strands. Usually mild mannered and accessible, he can be impatient and is known to lose his temper now and then. At the moment his face is passive, a faint smile around his lips as he listens to those present.

At the other end of the table sits the grandmother. A tiny, corpulent woman she wears a pleased, self-satisfied expression— as well she might. Her husband may be the Grand Rabbi in town, but she is the undisputed boss of her household. What she says goes — she rules with an iron hand. A pious woman, she is an indifferent homemaker — walking about with her prayer book for hours each morning. Nothing gets done until her prayers are finished. She is very self-possessed, with a sense of humor likely to turn into sarcasm and without a trace of anxiety about her. The grandfather treats her with deference and he, in turn, may be the only one whose needs she fully attends to.

The rest of the family present, three sons and a daughter, occupy the remaining chairs around the table. Uncle David is holding forth in his usual style, presiding over the meeting. The oldest son of the grandparents and the father of Sheinda's Cousin Tova, he is the recognized heir of his father and esteemed by the community. He holds no pulpit in this town, but has a post, reflected in his title, as the rabbi of an adjoining community. He and his family live here, however, in a house near the main synagogue.

Next to him sits his sister Chana Rachel, a young matron with two little children. She and her family live here in the house with the parents where they occupy a small suite of rooms. Chana Rachel resembles her mother both in stature and temperament. She is short, stout and easygoing, but is better natured than her mother: she is the one who sees to things when the grandmother is otherwise occupied. There are two other people in the room: Uncle Elazar and Uncle Simon. The former is a young man engaged to be married who still lives at home. He is engaged to his niece, the daughter of his oldest sister. They live across the border, which is why the wedding has not yet taken place. Uncle Simon, the youngest son of the family, is only about twenty. He is a rather obese, extroverted youth full of confidence and ambition. He is thought to be brilliant, a genius some think — but doesn't apply himself in formal study. He is always occupied with one communal project or another, always busy. Three other sons (including the young girl's father) and a daughter (Uncle Elazar's mother-in-law to be) live out of town.

As Sheinda enters the room her Uncle David is saying, "Of course, we don't know for certain; there are no absolutely reliable facts, but the rumors are very disturbing. Whatever goes on there isn't good! The question is what can we do to avoid it?"

"Can we go into hiding somewhere?" the grandfather asks.

"Some people have had the foresight to arrange something for themselves," Uncle David replies, "It takes trustworthy gentile friends and a lot of money to make it worth their while. We have neither and we're running out of time!"

The girl coughs, making her presence known. They hadn't noticed her coming in through the open door.

"Well, whom do we have here?" Uncle Elazar asks as he approaches her with a broad grin. "So you are passing through, are you?"

They turn toward her in welcome. She makes her way to the grandfather and kisses his proffered hand — a formality required of the grandchildren — then goes to hug the grandmother and aunt.

Her Uncle David sits immersed in thought, barely seeming to notice her. She is used to that attitude: while his wife, her Aunt Ruchtcha [Rachel], not to mention her cousin, their daughter, are exceedingly friendly and outgoing, he has always seemed remote; even condescending. "Why doesn't he ever smile when he sees me?" She used to wonder, "Why doesn't he speak to me? Doesn't he like me?"

She felt hurt and self conscious around him. It comes as something of a surprise therefore when he addresses her suddenly:

"How long have you been away from home?" he asks.

"About six weeks!" she replies.

"Do your parents know you are coming?"

"Yes, they are expecting me!"

"I suppose you do want to go home — you have been away for a long time?"

"I can hardly wait — I miss them so! — I'm glad to be here though, to see everyone. Can Cousin Tova come visit tonight?"

"I'm afraid that won't be possible — we've arranged for your cousin to go into hiding and she left last night! It may not be a bad idea for you to consider. You aren't registered. The authorities don't know you're here, won't be looking for you!"

"Tova in hiding — I won't get to see her after all. I was looking forward to our meeting, to talk about things," Sheinda is thinking: "my reliable cousin, the best of sisters, teachers, actually." Yes, Tova had filled that role for her — told her about things a growing girl needed to know. She hadn't realized until this moment how much she had counted on meeting with her.

"Of course, I cannot guarantee that it will work. I cannot state categorically that this is the way to escape. It's merely my advice. I will give you the information you'll need to contact Tova sometime in the future."

Categorically? Uncle David is using one of his fancy words. She never heard that one before; doesn't know its exact meaning but she does understand his advice — knows what he is trying to tell her: that she must remain separated from her family after all! Must again assume the burden of being alone!

"Thank you, Uncle David," she says, gratified by his evident concern, and leaves the room.

Next morning after breakfast she sits at the table dejected. She thinks about Uncle David's advice; about her cousin's absence, about the new challenge all this presents. She thought she had solved her problem, had been so happy on the way here: her resolve to return home taken, anticipation of reunion sweet, beckoning. Now her resolve is all but shattered!

"Oh, why is this happening to me? Why am I so indecisive, so incapable of making up my mind?"

The prospect of joining up with Tova, the two of them hiding out together ... the prospect has attraction, yes. But should she? What about her parents, her siblings; isn't her primary responsibility to them? What if she did manage to hide only to be caught and sent away alone...? Wouldn't that be too bad? Then again, maybe she would escape...? Still, it is her life! She wants to go home, she will go home!

"A penny for your thoughts." It was Uncle Simon speaking. "We are a bit glum today, aren't we? Whatever is bothering you? Might I be able to help? I would like to try, but first I want you to listen to this!"

He takes the book of Psalms he has been leafing through; finds the page he wants and proceeds to translate several verses from Hebrew into perfect grammatical German. [As far as she knew Uncle Simon never attended any formal secular school. Where did his knowledge of German — complete with the poetic expressions he uses — come from? Jews in these parts spoke

Yiddish, not German. It was obviously part of some project of his; a course of study he himself designed and executed.]

The verses he has chosen speak of one's helplessness in the face of death and fearlessness after committing one's soul to the care of the Almighty. Sheinda is fascinated. He manages to take her mind off her melancholy ruminations. She smiles at him.

"Now, if you wish, we can talk about your problem," He leads her out and they sit down on the landing at the top of the stairs leading to the cellar.

"I think you should stay here" he says softly, almost in a whisper. "You're so young, your entire life's ahead of you. Don't you think you should try?" —

"I can't, I'm so tired of being alone," she protests.

"You must try! Tova is doing it — haven't you heard? I am thinking about it, I haven't figured out how yet, but somehow I will manage to think of a way. If we succeed, the three of us, I mean, we will have each other! So you see, I think it's the right thing for you to do!"

"But what about …."

"I was coming to that! I suspect there isn't much chance you will be left together with them anyhow! There are rumors that they separate the families. We do know for certain that they are sending young people to work, don't we? We will be separated anyway, only much worse — we will be in their clutches."

How sad it all sounded, how threatening — how terribly disturbing. Her expectations of reunion, of being together with her loved ones, not possible after all.

"Ought I seek a way out?" she asks herself. "The way Uncle Simon is suggesting? Cousin Tova is doing it… instead of being alone, since they are breaking up families… we might be together, help each other, as he said."

Uncle Simon has long been the object of childish fantasy between the cousins and their playful competition for his attention. They both knew, had heard it discussed, that there weren't going to be many eligible girls around when time came for him to marry. She recalls one particular exchange:

"You know what I think?" Tova said to her young cousin one day. "I think it will be either you or me — one of us will wind up marrying him!"

"Marry whom? What are you talking about?" she asked.

"Uncle Simon, of course. One of us is destined to marry him!"

"It'll probably be you then," Sheinda said. "You're older and he admires you so — he always talks about how bright you are!"

Indeed, he wasn't the only one to admire Tova. Wasn't everyone raving about how capable, how exceptional, how brilliant and perfect she was? It used to annoy Sheinda no end to stand around and listen to such discourse, no one even realizing that she was a person too; that she may have some feelings, some expectation to hear her own capabilities praised. But no, that hardly occurred to them. Of course, she herself had to acknowledge, albeit grudgingly, Tova's unusual gifts.

Though perhaps not as gifted as Tova, she knew she too was bright, with many talents and capabilities. Her teachers often praised her for her originality and her resourcefulness. But she had her drawbacks: she didn't excel at everything and her vanity at times prevented her from making the most of the things she could do. An example would be the time when the grandfather, on his way to the large synagogue, suddenly decided to make an unexpected visit to the house of his oldest son, Uncle David and his family. Sheinda had been in town visiting and as always when they were in town, stayed at her cousin's house. It was Saturday morning and the girls, their prayer books in hand, were reciting the customary Sabbath morning prayers. Entering the room and seeing his granddaughters with their prayer books, the grandfather stopped and decided to listen in. He approached the girls in turn, bent his ear to the task and asked each to recite aloud in order to follow their progress. Tova did as she was ordered and came away with much praise.

Sheinda, on the other hand, found something of a dilemma in the situation: she was a year younger than her cousin and therefore a year short in practicing her Hebrew reading. Although her reading was quite good, she knew she could not match the fluency of her cousin. Instead of doing the best she could and showing her competence, she decided to remain silent, not read at all thereby giving the impression that she hadn't mastered the text at all. The grandfather stood there bending over her, trying to give her a chance, but didn't hear a thing and went away convinced that she hadn't learned to read at all! Perhaps there was something threatening in the situation that intimidated her, and prevented her from putting her best foot forward. It may have been the grandfather himself, something in his expression, betraying perhaps lack of expectation that put her off. She was a very sensitive child. It wasn't the last time her vanity or lack of confidence stood between her and her better judgment. In giving her opinion concerning who will marry Uncle Simon, however, Sheinda was influenced by her admiration for her cousin.

"But you're prettier — he will fall for your looks!" countered Tova, "And he likes you," she teased, "he will wait for you!"

"Not likely," Sheinda replied, "he will choose you, I know it!"

She had only the faintest idea what marriage and the physical union it entails meant. Only what Tova, more sophisticated about the facts of life, managed to impart. It all sounded fantastic and mysterious to her — incredible really, but with the strange appeal and excitement of anticipated experience.

"Think about what I said!" It was Uncle Simon speaking again, bringing her back to the present. "I suggest that you postpone your return for a while, to give yourself a chance — to think about the possibilities. You can always return home later, if that's what you decide to do."

Return later? What if...? Still, he had a point, Uncle Simon did.... She looked at him, meeting his frank gaze. His eyes were round brown orbs much like her father's, only more lustrous, alive with the vigor of youth, enveloping, disarming her. She wanted to protest, but was helpless against the force of his appeal. What was it that made his plan so attractive, that drew her like a magnet against her firm decision of yesterday and her better judgment of today? She sat there in confusion, then rose slowly deciding to give the matter more thought. Yes, she would think about it, give it a few days, as he suggested.

One morning the front door opened admitting Sheinda's little sister, Tzipora. Tzipora was a girl of about nine with long wavy blond hair arranged into thick braids, large blue eyes ringed with thick lashes, a small nose and a mouth with beautifully curving lips. She had her mother's coloring but her father's features.

Tzipora is the fourth child of her family. Although she is vivacious and intelligent she is overshadowed by her siblings — especially her two brothers: Samuel, slightly older than Tzipora and David, the baby of the family. In school Tzipora faced yet another challenge:

"Are you going to be as good a student as your sister?" her teacher had asked on the first day of school. The result was a less diligent, if not less capable, pupil. She lacked ambition to excel; wasn't as driven as her sister and brothers.

The two girls flew into each other's arms — crying and hugging each other for a long time.

"What are you doing here?" Sheinda asked.

"I came on an errand," her sister explained.

"Father has taken all our valuables together and I brought them. He wants grandfather to put them away for us. Here is your knapsack," Tzipora adds, handing her a blue bag made of coarse denim.

"Mama made them — we each have one and she wants you to have yours."

Sheinda took the knapsack and examined it carefully. It had several compartments, in addition to pockets on the front and the sides. She opened it and saw that it was stocked with a change of clothing, underwear and socks as well as a host of necessities such as soap, a comb, toothbrush and paste, Band-Aids and aspirin. In one pocket there was also a metal bowl with a spoon and fork. Although home made, the bag looked professional. She could see her mother's standard of work in its detail. Her mother made it with love, didn't spare her energy.

"Mama was rushing them, we don't have much time. She wanted them to be ready with all necessary things in them."

"Thank you for bringing it. How long are you staying?"

"I'm returning tomorrow — just as soon as grandfather is finished with his instructions for Father. Why don't you come home with me too?"

"Huh? Oh — yes, of course! I intend to! I'm thinking about it; I mean we will talk about it."

The very next day, true to her word, Tzipora is standing ready with her little valise, waiting for the bus to take her back home. Sheinda, her dilemma unresolved, tries to persuade her sister to remain with her.

"I have a suggestion," she says. "I was thinking — perhaps you ought to stay here with me for a while, don't you think? Maybe we can get away — hide somewhere? What do you think?"

"Oh no! Not me! Never! You wouldn't think of it either if you saw Mama!"

"What do you mean if I saw her?"

"I mean how sad she is, how broken up about you not being home! Why, she walks about crying all the time, she wants you home so very much! I want to tell you something; I can't understand you! How can you do this? I would never do what you're doing — no, never!"

Sheinda stands there taken aback, astonished by the resolute tone and firm behavior of her sister, a mere child, who speaks with such conviction and acts with such determination. The contrast between her sister's firmness and her own vacillation is shocking, unsettling to her; it reminds her of her former resolve. Is her present hesitation selfish, betraying lack of character? She doesn't know. She feels ashamed, but helpless in the face of her sudden need to wait!

Realizing that no amount of arguing will move Tzipora from her firm conviction, she gives in gracefully. The sisters embrace, say a hurried goodbye and the bus, carrying Tzipora, leaves town.

Sheinda is often haunted by the image of her sister: — this little girl standing there, her chin firmly set, looking back at her reproachfully. "You're my older sister!" she seems to be saying. "You ought to be teaching me! Don't you know any better? Do I have to tell you what is right?" An unforgettable challenge that, and from such a young child! Yes, the image haunts her and she wonders about the defensibility of her own choice at that fateful crossroads of her life.

At any rate, she had resolved to wait, hoping to look around; to find a place — some people who might hide her. The longer she stayed, the more she fell under the sway of her elders who counseled the course she was now following. She waited until there was no longer any choice, for one day, after breakfast, she found out that her family back home: her mother, her siblings and her old grandmother who lived with them had been taken away, shipped to Poland. Only her father, ill at the time, had been allowed to remain behind for a very short while, after which he too had been deported. He went alone, heartbroken, unsuccessful in his attempt to join her, his only child left to him, — to hide together — as he had intended.

Her only confirmation that she may have acted properly came a few weeks later from her mother. One day a postcard arrived — one of those official cards the Germans, anxious to conceal the true nature of the deportations, allowed to go through. The card was stamped with the name of a Polish village to which her family was brought.

My Dear Child,

I am writing to let you know that we are in this village called Rajovice, near Chelmno, in the vicinity of Lublin, we are told. The peasants who lived here in this hut were evacuated so that we could be herded in here. The place is impossible to describe. It is getting very cold here and the children, who are also hungry, are crying all the time. You remember how finicky they were always about their food, how difficult it was to make them eat? Not here! They are constantly begging for food and I have nothing to give them. Until recently I was able to trade with the peasants. I would give them a featherbed, a pillow or a coat for a piece of bread. I was luckier than some in that I was allowed to bring some things from home. But I am running out of things to trade with. May the Almighty help us — not keep us long in this place! — I am very happy to know that you are still at home. It gives us some hope that perhaps you may be able to do something for us — help us in some way! May God bless you and be with you!

Your loving mother,
HSH.

She was shaken by the postcard, and by the other two that followed a few weeks later. The first one had arrived in June, the last one in early August. That was it; she heard no more. She

33

carried them around wherever she went, reading and rereading the short missives. She was glad to have heard from her loved ones, glad to read the messages, for regardless of the sad content these words were actually written by her mother's hand. The neat little cards, moreover, so ordinary in appearance, carrying muted messages in which the worst of the conditions was carefully concealed did constitute some contact. They created the illusion, at any rate, that contact, and perhaps assistance was possible.

The grandfather immediately flew into a frenzy of activity. He was bothered by the fact that no word had arrived from his other children. He tried to send money and packages to them at the various places in Poland. Much later it turned out of course that none of that assistance had ever been allowed to reach its destination. At the time, however, the postcards represented hope and justification, to her, for having chosen to remain behind. Didn't her mother say so herself? Perhaps it would be possible for her to aid them in some fashion? Maybe she was meant to be the instrument of bringing them relief? Who knows, this might well be the reason she is being preserved! If she only could, how she would love to come to their aid, help her mother in her terrible need.

CHAPTER FOUR
MAMA

She can see her standing there: Mama, a very slender, almost gaunt figure clad, as always, in dark clothes. Her blouse has buttons high up to her throat. She wears a long skirt, black stockings and a pair of polished leather shoes. Her head is covered by a peculiar navy blue headdress that fits snugly around her clean-shaven head. A piece of brown silk protruding from the headdress onto her forehead is intended to suggest the fall of hair. ("Mama, where is your hair? Why have you no hair, Mama?" she would ask repeatedly during the years of her childhood. Much later her mother had explained: her wavy blond hair was cut off and her head shaven clean on the morning after her wedding-night. The hair was never allowed to grow back again. The girl had often tried to picture her blue-eyed mother with lovely blond hair — in place of the headdress she now wore — falling over her shoulders, but was unable to sustain the image for long. She had never seen her mother with her hair; the headdress became ingrained, part of her mother's image.)

She sees the very light somewhat pale complexion and smooth skin without any visible blemish. Her mother looks neat and well-groomed; a woman in her mid-thirties who knows her presence differs from that of other women but who has taken some pains with her appearance.

The girl sees her mother as she emerges from the bedroom her parents share. It is a large room, the largest in their house. At the far end of this spacious room, facing the door through which one enters, is the wall with the two enormous windows that look out onto the street below. Much light and sunshine find their way into the room through these windows. But neither the sunshine outside nor the heat within can do away with the moistness of the walls in the room. Indeed, the wet walls are a feature of the entire house and diminish considerably its neat and cozy aspect.

Between the two windows against the middle of the wall stands the blond, wooden toilette table with the large oval-shaped mirror in front of which Mama spends much time arranging her attire. On each side of the mirror stand the two twin beds — each at one extreme end of the wall with the windows — extending vertically toward the center of the room. Along the wall to the right from the entrance, a few feet from the foot of one of the beds, stands the large armoire with most of the household linen. Next to each of the beds is a nightstand holding washing utensils. In the center of the room is a largish table and chairs. A crystal vase holding an arrangement of faded silk flowers and a well-worn rug on the wooden floor complete the furnishings.

The bedding is a mixture of both the primitive and the luxurious. On the one hand, coarse sacks filled with straw take the place of mattresses in the beds. The straw has to be changed periodically to ensure cleanliness. On the other hand, these primitive straw sacks are covered with clean linen sheets of fine quality and the pillows and featherbeds — usually covered with beautiful hand embroidered linen — are stuffed with the finest goose-down produced at home. The brocade bedspreads have seen better days: they are worn and faded but the two large throw pillows — one at the head of each bed — of burgundy velvet and pink satin are custom made by Mama and retain something of their original richness and beauty.

On the left wall of this bedroom, opposite the armoire, is a door leading to another little room used as a combination bed and utility room. In the spring and summer months Sheinda uses this room as her private bedroom. It is from its vantage position that she is now observing. In this little room she has spent many an hour beautifying... wishing to turn it into a cozy place, without much success. The bed is an iron cot with a "straw sack" for a mattress. The bare walls, though painted with a pretty pattern of a contrasting color imposed on the paint, are damp. Besides the cot there is only a small wooden table and chair and a drab bookcase against the wall across from the bed. Nevertheless, she remembers the happy hours she spent here: storing and arranging her private books and school materials, doing her homework, reading and thinking.

The room has another advantage; it adjoins the bedroom of her parents, providing the illusion of company — the sense of not being alone. She loves to be lulled to sleep by the hum of their voices.

Of course, at times she can also hear strange sounds and disquieting language — discourse she would rather she hadn't heard! Like on that night she hasn't forgotten...is likely to never forget!

It was quite late, perhaps the middle of the night. She is awakened by strange whisperings coming from her parents' room. It sounds in fact as though the voices are coming from her mother's bed! Her father in her mother's bed...how on earth can that be? Why, they always maintain such scrupulous physical distance — hardly ever even touching each other! No, she cannot believe it...it must be a dream! But presently, her mother's bed begins to creak, groaning under their weight as they toss around in it, emitting peculiar sounds. How incredible! She sits up, toying with the idea of opening the door a crack — to look in, to see — but she hesitates, something is giving her pause...she decides against it; she doesn't want them to know she has heard!

Sometimes her parents would be taking stock, assessing their possessions, including their children: Lying in bed one night, on the verge of sleep, she overhears the following dialogue:

"Well, we are pretty fortunate, all things considered — I mean as far as the children are concerned — don't you agree?" her mother asks.

"Yes, I will say that is true, generally speaking — although they are, of course, not cut of identical cloth! There are considerable differences between them, as you know!"

What follows is a classification of their children into a hierarchy based on their personal (intellectual and behavioral) traits. She is dismayed — no, shocked, — to find that in their scheme of things she is being placed close to the bottom of the scale!

"She is a bright child; has a fine capacity for learning, we know that!" says her mother. "Her problem, I think, is lack of maturity for her age. This accounts for her temper, and why she has been so rebellious."

"I agree! She has a lot of growing up to do! But I am confident she will fall in line. It's a matter of time with her."

"Well, thank God for little favors! At least they didn't completely give up on me!" she thinks, her face flushed with embarrassment. She is strangely hurt by their unflattering image of her (compared to the rave accorded two of her brothers). She decides never

again to listen in, sensing that she cannot handle comments even mildly disparaging to her.

In the wintertime, because the room she sleeps in has no heating and is rather cold, she is glad to sacrifice privacy for warmth and sleeps in a heated bedroom with the other children. During the coldest winter months this, her private bedroom, is in fact utilized for housing the fowl: chickens and geese mostly, to prevent them from freezing in the exposed coops in the woodshed where they are otherwise kept.

She sees her mother, as she so often did, emerge from her bedroom and enter the narrow, longish hall that is the entranceway to their dwelling. The door leading into the house is to Mama's right. At the other end from the door is a window. The wall facing Mama leads to what they call a family room. It is a rather small room. Against one of the narrow walls (to the left of the door) there is a divan above which hangs a dark tapestry denoting a forest scene with some deer in it. In the corner of that same narrow wall stands a small iron wood burning stove providing heat for that wing of the house. Between the stove and the door (along the same long wall in which the door is), stands the daybed, providing sitting space during the daytime and a bed at night. Here in this room is where the children sleep. There are five of them: three boys and two girls and except for the youngest one, a boy, they sleep two to a bed; the divan serving as lodging for the two older boys, while the girl and her sister share the daybed. Along the wall opposite the door stands a crib, providing sleeping space for their baby brother.

Further down that same wall is a cupboard with glass doors, holding a sparse amount of family books, glassware and silver. The narrow wall to the right of the door has the window with a view into the courtyard and in the corner, to the left of the window, there is a cupboard for hanging clothes.

The table and chairs in the center of this room is where the family take their meals during the Sabbath and on the holidays. Otherwise the children eat either in the kitchen together with the adults, or at a special children's table with benches that stands between the entrance door and the window in the front hall.

The kitchen is a small area behind the partition-wall (opposite the main entrance to the house) separating the kitchen from the entrance hall. This wall is made of wood and has a large glass paneled double door in the center of it. It is through this door that one enters the kitchen, and it is here that Mama is now headed.

Facing her as she enters the kitchen is the long wall that has a kitchen cupboard, or kredenz — that extends to the far end of the wall adjoining the family room. The kredenz is white. It has a closed lower cupboard with shelves holding pots and pans, and an upper, hutch-like section with glass doors holding the china and crockery. In the center of the wall that adjoins the family room is a kitchen table made of wood, at each end of which are two square low kitchen stools. The kitchen cupboard and table and chairs are white, except for the tops, which are of natural wood.

High up the other extreme end of the wall holding the cupboard is a small window situated above the piekelik (the built-in drywall extension of the hearth) which forms the best kind of window seat possible. Warm in the winter and alight with sunshine most of the year it is cozy; the favorite place among the children. Here Sheinda spends many hours reading. The hearth is in the center of the narrow wall opposite that of the table (to the left of the double doors) and is built of bricks. It has a large iron platform on top that serves as a stove and a giant oven underneath. Under the oven is the opening with the grate in which to pile up the wood for building the fire.

Mama gets up at dawn. She is careful as she moves about not to disturb the children. Though they will have to be awakened soon she wants to get the fire started so the house will be warm when they rise.

Presently Mama disappears from view, but the girl soon hears her open the front door. She must be walking to the woodshed, where she will carefully select a bit of kindling and an armful of wooden logs cut to fit the small stoves. Returning, Mama starts the fires first in the children's room then in the kitchen. This can often be difficult; it requires careful arranging of the kindling and much patience with the addition of the logs which, often wet, smolder and smoke before they burn. It takes her some time to get a satisfactory fire going. When she emerges her face is flushed and red from exertion and her eyes smart from the smoke, but she has succeeded. Satisfied, she returns to the kitchen where with the help of Maña, their servant girl, she commences to prepare breakfast and lay the groundwork for the other labors of the day.

Much as she would like to linger, Sheinda decides it is time to get out of bed. By the time she and the other children have gotten up, her mother and the maid have managed to heat up the oven in the kitchen, haul in water from the neighborhood well, prepare and bake the homemade bread, cook breakfast — a hot cereal with some milk and fresh bread with margarine and coffee.

The coffee the children drink with their bread is a version of café au lait — half a cup of coffee made from chicory with a lot of skimmed milk and sugar. The milk is neither homogenized nor Pasteurized and has to be boiled. Before she does so, Mama skims most of the cream off the top and sets it aside for butter and cream. Occasionally she also sets aside a portion of the milk with the cream still on top for what becomes "sour milk," a sort of yogurt or leben, a great favorite with the children. Today Mama is boiling a bit of whole milk, as she sometimes does. Because it is not homogenized, the cream rises to the top and has to be carefully removed from the fire before over-boiling. When it cools, boiled whole milk forms a thick creamy crust on top, which can be used as a spread for the bread. Mama's home-baked bread, topped with the delicious crust from the boiled milk, is a special treat.

Sheinda is dressing in a hurry now, the tantalizing aroma of the food filling her nostrils, the expectation of it making her mouth water.

After the children are dressed, have eaten and gone off to school, Mama turns her attention to the rest of the day's work. That includes walking to Main Street along which the peasants from adjoining villages have formed a marketplace — as they do twice each week — displaying and selling their produce. That market is the place where Mama obtains most goods for her table: poultry, fish, fruits, vegetables, fresh eggs and other provender. Here she must first select the merchandise — a complicated procedure in the case of chickens, roosters, geese and ducks — which she must carefully examine after which comes the lengthy haggling with the peasants until a satisfactory price has been reached. Mama doesn't just buy what she wants when she finds it; she surveys all that is available — settling finally on what seems the best buy for the money. She must stretch her available funds.

Today Mama has invited her young daughter to accompany her to the market! The girl makes good use of the time there. While her mother is busy choosing her fowl, she wanders around the market fascinated by the multitude of people and the vast array of produce displayed.

She meets one of her friends and together they inspect every stall and gorge themselves on the abundant fresh fruit and vegetables: sweet red plums, delicious pears, apples and homegrown tomatoes. They circle the tables of the vigilant peasants and manage, by and by, to pilfer a good deal.   There are loads of delicious tomatoes — freshly picked, sweet as sugar, and they help themselves repeatedly when the owners aren't looking!

"Well, I think it's time to go!" Sheinda finally says to her friend. They part and she turns to the task of locating her mother, whom she finds still immersed in her transactions. Mama lacks decisiveness — (a trait her daughter inherited). She can't make up her mind which hen or goose is the best.

Finally back at home, after both their large baskets are emptied, Maňa proceeds to the schochet— the ritual slaughterer who kills the poultry for today's meal, a pair of young hens. These have to be plucked, opened, cleaned and "made kosher," a process of soaking, salting and rinsing after allowing the salt to drain the blood. The poultry must then be scalded to remove all remaining feathers and stubble. Only then is Mama ready to cook the meal, which is nevertheless ready when the children arrive home for dinner at one o'clock.

By the time they arrive the table has been set: there is fresh bread, bowls of steaming vegetable soup, generous portions of roasted chicken enlarged by stuffing under the skin, roast young potatoes (brought in from the cellar which Mama grew in their garden — the fenced-in plot of land in the yard — along with beans, cabbage and tomatoes) string beans, pickles and a freshly baked sponge cake, complete today's menu. Dinner is their only elaborate meal of the day and Mama makes sure it is nourishing and appetizing.

The meal is over but Mama's daily work continues. She must see to it that the table is cleared, the dishes washed and stored, the poultry just obtained, that is to last for the rest of the week and some of it beyond, locked in their coups and fed, supper prepared and the washing, ironing, darning and sewing for the family seen to. She must also prepare the Sabbath foods that must be planned for ahead of time: the noodles, farfel and challah are examples of these and they must all be handmade at home. There are also the labors connected with special seasonal foods: preparing and canning of fruits, vegetables, relishes and preserves that must be cooked in the summer and stored up for the winter months. During the fall and winter seasons Mama also fattens poultry, mainly geese, for the rendered fat they yield.

Although she has a number of assistants, in addition to the permanent presence of Maňa, she has workers who come in regularly for special tasks: (a washer-woman, house-cleaner, and kitchen maid) she is constantly occupied, her work never ending. Their home lacks modern conveniences: The house has no central heat, water, or electricity and therefore no refrigeration; no inside toilet or bath; no dishwasher or vacuum cleaner; no ready supply of conveniently packaged foods or kitchen necessities available in the local store.

But Mama runs a clean, well-ordered household and under her circumstances that means constant hard work to which she brings devotion and love. No, Mama has no complaints. She derives much satisfaction from her labors. She is the type who cannot sit idle, is seen rushing around the house constantly organizing, arranging and seeing to it that all is in order and on schedule. She enjoys the work itself, but mainly it is the means to her main goal in life: to provide a wholesome environment for her family — an environment in which her husband and children are able to pursue the ways of Torah. She seems to have very few other interests to interfere with this main goal and none in terms of personal needs she might consider placing above those of her family.

One of her great worries concerns her health. She has had gallstones for many years and she often gets very ill: so ill in fact that she turns yellow; suffers excruciating pain which can only be stilled with morphine; and is confined to her bed — often for a number of days — prostrate with inertia and oblivious to everything around her. She knows there are some cures. One possibility is surgery, of course, but she firmly rejects that alternative. She is not going "under the knife." So she undertakes periodic "cures" — mainly home or quack remedies which are believed to have removed stones without resort to surgery.

Currently Mama is under a cure that requires the consumption of gallons of heavy oil, a glassful at a time, and her daughter watches as she is putting herself through its excruciating routine. She drinks the thick liquid slowly, a gulp at a time (eager to prevent *vomiting the stuff she has forced down) with purpose and optimism. Anything to avoid the attacks that cause her so much suffering; anything short of surgery that is, for surgery is the one thing she will not contemplate.*

In between the feared attacks there is also something they have come to know as "pressure," a much milder form of the malady: a relentless, though not acute pain brought on by even the slightest deviation in her strict diet. (Often her very cures, for example the oil cure described above, will bring on the feared attack.) For this reason she must wear a flannel girdle, both summer and winter, which she believes eases the pressure somewhat.

Today Mama succeeded in downing the oil without much difficulty and looks pleased. She takes all of this in stride. Her chronic illness doesn't keep her from diligently performing her manifold duties — the exception being those feared attacks which totally incapacitate her but over which she has no control. She prays to the Almighty with much devotion to remove this affliction from her.

Mama's time for prayer is the late afternoon (Mincha) service for which she makes time every day, and does so now. The young girl looks at her mother as she stands there now — prayer book in hand, head lowered into the pages of the open book, her closed eyes filled with burning tears. There is nothing perfunctory about this performance; though it is regular, routine, it has always been marked by extraordinary fervor, as it is now. "What is Mama praying for?" Sheinda wonders. "Is it about her illness? Yes, probably her illness," she concludes, but certainly not only that! Mama has other cares. Her illness is not her only nor even her main concern during these sessions with the Almighty. No, Mama directs her supplication toward her main goal in life — to be the instrument; to be allowed to lead her family toward the service of God....

After her prayer, Mama's mood lifts. She has great faith in the Almighty. Surely He knows her heart — He must know that whatever her shortcomings, for which she is being punished through her illness, they are not intentional. She begs for favor only to be able to fulfill His will.

Mama's demeanor left a lasting impression. Not so much in moving her daughter — who stood there watching intently — to emulate her mother's behavior, as in convincing her that her mother is an extraordinary individual: a woman of sincerity and of great humility.

PART II

FALL: 1942

ESCAPE

CHAPTER FIVE
DEPORTATION

On the morning of the dreaded day, when all Jews in the community are forced to vacate their dwellings and are herded into and around the synagogue — there to await their imminent departure from town — Sheinda silently walks toward the yard of the neighbor adjoining her grandparents' house. She climbs across the narrow fence separating the two courtyards and finds her way to the woodshed in the back of the yard at some distance from the house.

It is a small square room with a tiny window high up on one of the walls. There is no door — the entrance through which she had entered the shed is a wide-open square in the wall, exposing the inside of the shed to view from outside. She makes her way into one corner of the shed, underneath the window, directly to the right of the entrance where she hopes she will be obscured from view and sits down on the damp ground. She closes her eyes and takes a deep breath to control her trembling and the wild beating of her heart. So far everything seems okay. She hopes no one had seen her cross the fence. Thank God there was no dog here — no barking to alert anyone! She keeps her eyes closed and rests.

Presently she opens her eyes and looks around. The shed holds neatly arranged piles of wood against its walls, the logs cut short to fit the size of the little iron stoves in the house. In the center of the room are various implements used in farming as well as much clutter   old and broken furniture and a heap of other unused things. Rising from among the stored clutter in the middle of the shed she sees a ladder leading to what appears to be a loft — a second story over one half of the shed. She carefully makes her way toward the ladder, climbs up to its last rung and steps into what looks like a bale of hay spread out over the wooden floor. Good...! This will be better to hide her from view and will provide some comfort from the damp ground on the lower level. She sits in the hay and inhales its aroma — then puts her head on her knees and begins thinking about what lies ahead....

Suddenly, coming from a distance, she hears the faint, familiar voice of her mother. Could it be? Mama calling her? Yes, it is her mother... the voice is unmistakable, but she isn't calling her — no, she is calling to the maid who is assisting her in the kitchen.

They are all at home.... It is early in the morning on a regular fall day. She is still in bed, relishing the few moments before jumping up to face the new day. She opens her eyes and through the open door follows her mother as she is making her way through the house.

There she is, Mama, dressed as always in her dark clothes, but her headdress is no longer there: no, instead, her hair is covered with some sort of gauze that glitters like a halo around her head. The girl jumps out of bed and moves toward her mother.

"Mama! Oh Mama!" she calls, but her mother gives no sign, no indication that she has heard....

"Oh, she is praying," the girl guesses. "She can hear me, but cannot respond; she isn't allowed to talk until she is done. I'll just wait here a while." She stops her advance and moves into the corner of the room, near the door, and sits down on the floor.

She sees that it is evening. Of course, time for Mama's Mincha prayer. Mama has moved toward the eastern wall, her face buried in her prayer book, her eyes lifted toward heaven; she is praying silently, without a sound. The girl cautiously moves from the door, positioning herself so as to see her mother's face and is touched. Mama's cheeks are streaked with tears that are falling still in little streams from her eyes.

"Oh, why is Mama crying so? Her heart is broken, I think." The girl sobs and moves toward her mother who turns around to look at her. Mama's eyes are now dry and the gentle smile around her lips has widened into a broad grin. She beckons to her daughter to come closer. When the girl is near enough her mother embraces her, then looks into her eyes with a lingering gaze and shining countenance. The girl is mesmerized...she stands there motionless as if nailed to the ground.

Suddenly, the lights have turned dim; the scene is receding. She is straining to recapture the familiar sight but, try as she may, is unable to do so. Her home, her mother, the entire surroundings are no longer there; they have disappeared...they are gone!

Sheinda opens her eyes and slowly looks around. It takes her a moment, but only a moment, to shake off the spell. Alas, it was only a dream! With a start she realizes where she is...! Oh, it is time she did something to conceal her whereabouts.... She cannot remain here, in this shed, not if she is to succeed! She makes her way to the edge of the loft and looks through the opening on the lower level, but all she can see is the sky. She sees that the sun is quite high; that much of the day is gone. Yes, she must think of some way, form some plan of action!

Presently she becomes aware of a constant hum — like a chorus of voices — in the background. What can that be...? Slowly she descends the steps and soon stands before the "door" of the shed looking out in disbelief! In front of her she beholds an incredible spectacle: The narrow path along the right bank of the creek leading to the "downs" is crowded by a long, never ending line of people of all ages. All of them are Jews; they carry bundles in their hands or on their backs and are followed by their children. They are hurried along by the uniformed guards with clubs in their hands.... Interspersed among them are the young Jewish men, those still in town, — wearing white armbands — carrying pails of water and helping along the young and the infirm. They are all on the way to the synagogue around which tents have been erected to accommodate the entire community. They come in streams from every direction in town, pouring into the narrow path in front of her, the path that leads to the synagogue! They are bewildered: their faces drawn and sad; their spirits flagging. They talk in muted voices but are unable to obscure the moans and wails emanating from every corner. She stands there as if glued to the spot, unable to move, overwhelmed by the grief before her.

She is sufficiently close to be able to recognize the people she knows and sees many familiar faces moving by. Among the young men with their white armbands, she recognizes the two sons of the family from across the street. She can hear them talk to each other, but cannot discern what they are saying. Presently one of them is helping a little girl who has tripped to get back on her feet. Sheinda strains to see the child's face, is able to do so clearly, but she doesn't recognize the little one.

She turns her face toward the oncoming line of people and freezes to the spot. There, in front of her, accompanying the new line of people is her Uncle Simon. He too has a white armband and he appears to be seriously engaged in the task before him. At the moment both his hands are occupied, he is carrying a pail — water presumably — in each of them, while seeming to answer questions, pacify children and allay fear of the adults who confront him. She is amazed at his transformation. He has not only taken on a new role, but his countenance has changed: His beard and side curls are gone! He is clean-shaven and is wearing a light colored suit instead of the traditional garb.

Uncle Simon here...together with all others to be taken away? She is amazed, disappointed and very sad. She didn't expect to see him here. What happened to his resolve? He was so certain, so convinced of what he must do, and her own action is largely the result of his firm belief that they must seek to save themselves. What happened to all that? Has his resolve to hide simply vanished in the face of this urgency; this need to help the others? Or is there some other explanation...? Could this be part of some plan he has formed? At the moment his entire attention and energy are taken up by the task at hand. While she is standing there observing, he has gone and returned several times — his arms loaded, his features set — determined to bring whatever comfort he could to the people he is assisting.

It is comforting to see him; to observe him secretly as he dispenses aid to those around him. She wants so to let him know where she is — that she is safe for the time being — but calling out to him is out of the question. She will have to wait! She must think...must form a plan of action and do it fast, before night — now fast approaching — descended!

She returns to her place in the loft, sits down in the hay and thinks.... What to do? What should be her next step? She cannot remain here for the night, can she? First of all, there is no real security here. Why, the shed doesn't even have a door! She is bound to be discovered soon, if not by the authorities, certainly by the owners! It is also becoming unpleasant here. The night is coming, bringing with it darkness, solitude and cold. And she is hungry... has had nothing to eat all day.

What to do? She could try to sleep in the hay for a while; could probably find something among the clutter below to cover herself with. That will take care of the cold and her exhaustion somewhat, but she is hungry and so afraid! No, it is better to act now...better to confront them before they discover her. Someone is bound to enter the shed soon! She must forestall that! She will show them her trust, disarm them with her helplessness — her dependence!

Suddenly, she hears a noise...a scratching...coming from the direction right in front of her. She peers through the dusk, straining to make out the source of the noise and is petrified with fear. In front of her is a little gray creature with a long tail and beady eyes. A mouse...or rat...perhaps? Oh, no! Not a rat! Please God! Please let it not be a rat! She trembles, looking around in panic for a place to hide and braces herself for a closer look at the creature. She decides it is too small to be a rat! It's a tiny mouse, one of those small animals she has often come across around the houses and fields. Still, to be caught in here with them, trapped...at their mercy all night! She is afraid, revolted, and remains glued to the spot trying to decide what to do about this new menace, when the creature scampers out of view, disappearing as suddenly as it appeared.

She sighs, wiping away the tears brought on by her sudden fright and decides that all things considered there really is no choice. She must confront the inhabitants of the house who own this shed. She waits until it is pitch dark outside then slowly makes her way into the yard....

As soon as she reaches the door she knocks, afraid to wait lest her courage should dwindle. The door springs open with a creak exposing an elderly woman in peasant attire. The girl recognizes her — it is the widow next door who lives in the house with her bachelor son.

"Good evening," she whispers softly. "I am the rabbi's granddaughter from next door! No one knows I am here, you see... if you could give me shelter for the night, I shall try to join my grandparents in the morning. My grandfather was given an exception, because he is the rabbi. He is allowed to remain. I was hiding in your shed since this morning...I hope you don't mind."

The woman stands listening to her without a word, then grabs her by the hand, pulls her into the hut and slams the door shut.

Sheinda finds herself in a large, dingy room smelling of bacon and cabbage. The table near one of the walls has not yet been cleared — it is piled with the empty dishes from their recent supper.

The woman brings down a clean plate from one of the shelves places on it a slice of black bread spread with butter. She fills a glass with milk and offers it all to the girl whom she has pushed into a chair at one end of the table. While Sheinda eats, the widow calls in her son; instructs him to see to lodging for himself in the woodshed. When the girl has finished eating, the widow makes up her son's bed, which stands in an alcove adjoining her bedroom, and tells the girl to undress. She helps her into bed, dims the lamp and exits.

Sheinda is overwhelmed with gratitude. She senses that it is the hand of God...what else can it be? She feels as though the entire day had been planned for her by some higher power; she merely seems to have followed it blindly — as if pushed into action by an invisible, benevolent hand.... She begins to recite her prayers silently but with great devotion, then turns to the wall and abruptly falls asleep.

The next day it is almost noon by the time Sheinda has made it out of bed. Her head aches and she feels nausea. She tries to eat some of the food the widow has placed before her, but finds that she cannot swallow a single bite. She pushes aside the plate, rising slowly and approaches the widow who is busying herself around the kitchen stove:

"I need a favor from you," she says softly but in a determined voice,

"I must send a message to my grandparents — to the rabbi and his wife next door! Do you think your son might go and take it to them? They should be informed that I am here!"

"I'm afraid my son can't do it! He has been in the field since early this morning, but I will go; give me the message."

She hands Sheinda the requested piece of paper and pencil and stands by silently watching her write. The girl scribbles a few lines on the paper, looks through it, then hands it to the woman saying:

"After you have delivered this message, will you be able to take another one for me? This one will be to another address that

I will give you later. No, wait! I think it is best for you to have it now. You can go there immediately after you have seen my grandparents."

She writes the second message, addressing it to her cousin, and scribbles the name of the family and address where it is to be taken, having memorized these details, then hands it to the widow. The latter takes a few moments, getting ready to leave. Before she is able to depart, Sheinda suddenly approaches and throws her arms around the widow's neck.

"I thank you," she murmurs. She wants to continue, but is choked by tears welling up within her. The widow just stands there rigidly for a few moments, then takes the notes and leaves the room.

The widow now makes her way across the yard, through the iron gate, into the adjoining courtyard linking her house with that of the rabbi's. She is apprehensive about her errand — she doesn't want to shock them and deliberates what might be the best way to bring them the news. She decides upon the direct approach: she will simply ring the bell, tell them who she is and let them know in as matter-of-fact a manner as possible that their granddaughter is in her house.

Immediately upon her arrival she rings the bell. Keeping her finger steady, she presses down a bit harder than usual, wishing the chime to do its job the first time around. She soon removes her hand and waits, listening for movement from within. She doesn't have long to wait. The rabbi and his wife have approached the door and are opening it slowly, with care — just a crack at first, then, seeing the widow from next door, they open it widely and bid her come in. She does so, relieved to see that they have recognized her: that makes her task a bit simpler.

She is taken aback at the sight of the old people. They are both pale and look haggard. The rabbi has a bandage over his right eye, covering part of his forehead and the right side of his head. The widow shows concern:

"I hope you're all right," she says, moving closer, her voice questioning — "is it very painful?"

"Not as painful as having to see all our children depart!" says the rabbi's wife. "They knocked him down, you see — he was running after the children; we thought our children were safe, but they wouldn't let them stay! Grown children aren't protected by the letter, they said. He pleaded with them but it did no good. They took a club to him and left him lying unconscious...I was relieved to find him alive!"

"I hope this will cheer you up" says the widow handing her the note she brought. The rabbi approaches, unfolds the note his wife has just handed him with a puzzled expression and reads in a hushed voice:

My Dear Grandparents,

I am glad to let you know that I managed to slip away yesterday. The widow and her son were brave; they ignored the danger. I think it is safe for us to communicate through them! I want to join Cousin Tova soon, but would like to come spend a few days with you first. Do let me know what you think; nobody is to know that I am here...! I hope you are both well — I'm waiting to hear from you.

I love you, your granddaughter S.

"Thank God," exclaims the grandmother. "At least one...this one child may be granted us, but it must remain a secret! No one may know." The rabbi walks over to the widow. He speaks, lowering his voice to a whisper:

"It is an extraordinary deed, what you are doing. I would like to thank you, but I know it isn't necessary — I'm certain you understand, God will thank you...!" He brings paper and pencil, writes a short message in answer to his granddaughter and hands it to the widow saying:

"May God bless you and your undertaking! I have written our child that we are expecting her as soon as you can arrange it to bring her over safely."

The widow takes her leave and hastens away. She has much to attend to, among her errands is the one to deliver the second message the girl has given her. By the time she will return home, it will be dark.

Sheinda has been awaiting the widow's return with great impatience. She has no doubt that her grandparents will approve her plan; what worries her is the prospect of joining her cousin in her hiding place. Oh, she knows her cousin will be happy, and so will she, but what about the people who shelter her cousin? So far no one has informed them of the plan for her to join Tova; will they approve? They don't even know her and no one has made arrangements for her; they may not have room for her....

Well, no use worrying over the matter, she will soon find out! She looks around the widow's quarters in search for something to do. She has never liked to sit around idly, but now, time hangs with particular heaviness on her hands. She decides to make the beds and wash the dishes that are piled up in a washbasin in a corner of the kitchen.

She looks around and locates the soap, dishcloth, scouring pad and a dishtowel — scattered in various places around the kitchen. She washes the dishes carefully, then dries them, and — not knowing where each item belongs, she places them all in a neat pile on one end of the table. She then makes her way to the bedroom. She fluffs the pillows and arranges them at the head of the bed. She looks around for the bedspread, locates it and after she straightens and tucks in the sheets and blanket she carefully covers the bed. She looks around the room, removes some stray pieces of paper from the floor, as well as the empty pitcher and glass from the nightstand. She then closes the door and reenters the kitchen.

She pulls a chair up to the window, and sits down — allowing her gaze to wander into the widow's yard and garden. It is late in the afternoon. The widow has been gone most of the day. She will be back soon, no doubt, provided nothing has gone wrong....

A streak of sunlight, filtering in through the faded curtain of the closed window, catches her eye. She pushes aside the curtain and looks out into the yard, allowing her gaze to drift toward the horizon. The sun is low now, about to set, a beautiful red ball in the sky surrounded by streaks of color, about to fall behind the distant hills.

She always loved the spectacle of the setting sun...but isn't sufficiently composed just now to appreciate its beauty. She is taken aback — surprised, really, that nothing at all seems to have changed in nature. The sun, the birds, trees and flowers — they are all around, unchanged, none of them giving the slightest indication of the turbulence going on in her life.... She moves away from the window and sits down at the table with her head resting gently on her hands and waits.

After a little while she hears footsteps approaching the house. She jumps up from the chair and moves toward the door, which opens presently, admitting the widow. The girl approaches her in anticipation.

"I'm so glad you're back" she says. "I was beginning to worry!"

"Oh, no need to worry, your grandparents seem well — and are glad to hear from you, very glad, indeed."

"Were they shocked to hear about me?"

"They were surprised — yes, in a pleasant sort of way." The widow makes no mention of their painful experiences; the girl will find that out soon enough!

"They are excited that you are here and that you will visit them. As soon as my son comes home tonight we shall make a plan to take you over there safely.

"Thank you!" Sheinda says. "Oh, have you spoken to my cousin? Were you able to find the place? I hope I gave you the correct address. I had to memorize it, you see, I worried while you were gone — I was afraid you may not find them!"

"No, no! I found them alright! That's not the problem!"

"Ah, is there a problem?"

"Yes, I'm afraid there is — a big problem!"

"Why, what do you mean?"

"Your cousin isn't there, my dear, that is the problem."

"Not there? You say she isn't there? But where is she? Where did she go?"

"It's very strange! You won't believe it! The girl, your cousin, I mean, she was all settled in — content, expecting to hear from you. She had been with them for quite a while and they were all getting used to her presence; had worked out some of the problems. But yesterday a note arrived from her father requesting her to come home! There was no indication why; they have no idea what caused him to change his mind. Your cousin was sad, but she obeyed her father and left! She is there with them now, in the synagogue, with all the others!"

The girl stands there in shock...she can't believe she had heard correctly; doesn't want to accept these tidings as the reality, as immutable fact that cannot be changed. She advances all sorts of ideas — to the widow at first, later in dialogue with herself — all in an effort of retaining some shred, some glimmer of hope that all isn't lost. She finally retreats to a corner of the bedroom and cries bitterly — her way of conceding...of acknowledging the facts. She will have to struggle on alone after all! Not only Uncle Simon, on whose presence she had pinned so much hope is gone from her life; Tova too is now gone! Tova, her wonderful friend, the one being who might have made reality endurable will not be with her. She will be all alone! She weeps as though she can never again be consoled, her loud sobs diminishing after intervals, only to be repeatedly renewed in intensity in successive outbreaks of weeping. This goes on until she is thoroughly exhausted, her crying subsiding at last into a soft whimper.

The widow leaves her alone and busies herself with the preparation of supper. Neither of them had eaten all day and soon her son, too, will be home — expecting his meal after a hard day's work. She works on quietly, keeping her ears tuned to the sounds from the next room.

When the girl seems sufficiently composed, the widow enters the room softly. "I know you've had a terrible disappointment" she says, "but I think you must now put all of that behind you and get ready for your visit — don't you agree?" She takes a handkerchief from her pocket and hands it to the girl.

"Yes, I know," murmurs Sheinda, "thank you!" She stands up, wipes her tears and allows the widow to lead her into the kitchen.

The house is quiet...so very, very quiet. It has been that way since her reunion with the old folks. Grandmother is out on an errand...a chore Sheinda herself would normally be expected to do, but circumstances have been anything but normal. Her presence must be carefully concealed: no one is to suspect it. She cannot leave the house, but even in the house it must be circumspect, confined to it's less exposed areas.

Sheinda misses the bustle of the adults and the noise of the children...all the sounds associated with this house that are no more! She opens a door, expecting to hear their arguments, shouts and laughter, but is met with an oppressive silence instead. Their voices, heard so recently, echo all around her, but nothing tangible remains...they are gone!

It is her task now to provide whatever comfort she can to her grandparents. She recognizes that to be her duty and tries to do so, but it isn't easy. Her grandparents are glad to have her, of course, but cannot be consoled — cannot accept the loss of their children and their other grandchildren. And she, while trying to console them, must struggle with her own grief! Where are her parents...her brothers...her little sister...her old grandmother who had lived with them? She knows where they had been taken, she wants to help them, but is at a loss how to go about it; what to do?

And her father...is another story of grief! He had been ill during the deportations in their town — perhaps feigning more severe illness than was the case, in the hope of obtaining an exception for himself and his family — but the gambit didn't work. He alone was allowed to remain behind. Alone, ill, dependent and emotionally broken, he was unprepared and unable to fend for himself.

He had written to her and together they devised a plan! She will come under the guise of a peasant girl...will rent a conveyance and bring him back hidden under a load of farm produce. She knew the plan was not without risk but was ready, indeed eager, to put it into action. Unlike the situation of the rest of her family, here was something tangible she could actually do to help save her father! And the plan provided her with something to do — some positive activity that had great appeal to her resourcefulness and her sense of adventure. Yes, the more she thought about it, the better the plan looked. She needed some funds and assistance from some local people in arranging for the horse and buggy she will need. But these were surmountable obstacles. It could all be arranged...! She was excited and presented the plan to her grandparents with resolve, if not enthusiasm.

"*You* will go to bring your father? In peasants' clothes? Dressed as a peasant girl, pretending you're carrying a load of goods to market? But you're too young for that! You will have to have someone else with you, some adult."

"I'll talk to the widow, she will do it — or, maybe her son-"

"No, better leave them out; they have done enough!"

"So who do we ask? The family that was to hide Tova, perhaps? They ought to be reliable; I think they might help!"

"Finding someone to go with you is not the main issue — there is another problem: You would be taking a very great risk. It is a question of safety! If they stop you on the way and begin asking questions, you will almost certainly be exposed and detained! And we would be arrested as well — your grandmother and I. No, much as I regret to tell you this, I cannot approve of this plan!"

"But father...what about *his* safety?! Aren't you concerned about him? He is your son and he depends on us!"

"Let me see if we can come up with some other way. I will think about it...consult with some of our people who have experience, some contacts."

The grandfather did contact some people, and various plans to bring her father over had been discussed, but nothing came of these...mainly, she suspected, because the grandfather was afraid to take the risk. She understood his fear, but was hurt — yes, resentful, at this sudden "excessive" caution. Hadn't she taken a risk to preserve herself? Didn't her own presence continue to be a daily risk? Why this caution where her father was concerned? Could it be that the grandfather loved him less...cared less about her father's than about her own well-being? These thoughts occupied many of her waking hours and stood like a wall between her and her grandparents.

A few weeks after the general deportation — in the course of which all Jews had been taken to the central location whence they were shipped to the East — several from among the wealthy Jews of the town had returned. They had been able to buy their way out; unlike the bulk of the deportees, they had been allowed to return home. Among them was Sander Weisman, a friend of the family, who came to see her:

"I saw your father," he told her. "He was glad to hear about you, but sad that you weren't there. I think he must have hoped for reunion with you. He wanted so very much to see you! He walked around asking everyone about you, your whereabouts, and cried when he realized that you weren't there, that you didn't come!"

This information vastly aggravated her ambivalence toward her grandfather. In her mind's eye she could see her father running around, asking about her; the only member of his immediate family still within reach, so to speak; the only one who might have eased his pain. The separation from her mother and the children had been a heavy blow. It had been unexpected and it broke his spirit. In his utter helplessness he longed for the comfort of having her beside him. He had clung to this last ray of hope, but this, too, had been denied him.

She understood his need and his bitter disappointment. Hadn't she, under less tragic circumstances, known the fear of being alone...the longing for togetherness and the pain of separation? She understood her Uncle David's desire to have his daughter around him a bit better now — in the light of her father's predicament. (In contrast, her mother's and her little sister's heroic acts loomed up before her in their true immensity! Here was utter selflessness. Her mother, too, had desired her presence — had wanted her home. But she withstood — she never mentioned it; never asked her to return. No, she had pushed her own needs into the background, thinking only of what's best for her daughter!)

Sheinda couldn't help feeling disappointed in the grandfather. His action vis-a-vis her father seemed somehow selfish, in disregard of her father's dire need! She felt resentful, blaming the grandfather for her failure to be reunited with, perhaps to have saved her father.

For a long while these feelings prevented the development of intimacy between Sheinda and her grandparents. She was obedient, complying with the demands of her peculiar situation; executing her daily chores as efficiently and lovingly as she could. But she couldn't help maintaining a certain reserve — a distance she attributes to her ambivalence.

CHAPTER SIX
SURVIVING

Thus the days follow one another. She does the household chores, including most of the kitchen work, while the grandmother goes shopping and does all of the outdoor errands. Sheinda has to be careful, refraining from opening the door in haste — as she had almost done on several occasions — but she is growing accustomed to caution and a bit bored by the routine. At times, during the evening hours, there are meetingd, either in there, or in some other jewish neighbors house. These meetings concern current problems — news about their loved ones; the grave peril they are in and their own precarious position. For the time being they are enjoying a bit of respite. The deportations from the town have stopped! For those who remained, there are the letters of protection, emphasizing their importance to the economy! But all of that is temporary. They know better than to sit and await their fate; at the mercy of the local and government officials. They are constantly devising plans...to be ready to put into action at a moment's notice! Everyone has a plan, and the grandfather is no exception. In the meantime, they have to be on guard — especially the young girl, whose residence with her grandparents is illegal.

The house is quiet, as usual. Sheinda is entering the kitchen, when she hears loud rapping at the door. She freezes...her heart pounding wildly. What to do? She mustn't be caught here...she doesn't know who it might be. The grandmother makes her appearance and silently motions toward the closet in the vestibule. The door of this closet opens into the vestibule — but it is obscured by a large cupboard that stands to the left of it and by a number of overcoats hanging on hooks mounted to it. To the uninitiated, it appears as though the coats are hanging from hooks on the wall. She opens the door silently and disappears into the dark closet. She sits down on the floor next to the wall and waits, trying to control the noisy beating of her heart.

The grandmother, in the meantime, has opened the door admitting someone. Sheinda hears voices, but the exchange isn't loud enough for her to make out what is being said. The speakers remain in the vestibule for some time, after which she can hear them making their way to the inside quarters of the house. She has no inkling who it is. She will have to remain here in silence — and darkness — for as long as necessary; awaiting directions from the grandmother.

Yes, it looks as though it will be a long and tedious day, but she isn't complaining. She is filled with a sense of gratitude for having had time to disappear undetected and is determined to pray — to implore the Almighty, who has been sheltering her in her hours of need.

She is sorry that it is so dark and that she has no prayer book! She will have to recite some of the prayers she knows by heart. She repeats the daily prayers, including the She'ma, with great fervor. A few verses of the Psalms, appropriate to the occasion, would be in order. She knows that there are verses designated for every occasion — including danger. But she isn't conversant with these! She will have to make up her own prayer...something that will address her present need.

She recalls the story her mother once told — of the illiterate shepherd boy who strayed into the synagogue during a Yom Kippur service. Wishing to be part of the congregation and of the prayers, but lacking the knowledge to do so, he picked up a prayer book, raised it toward heaven and whispered: "Dear God, I don't know how to pray, won't you please take the entire Siddur [prayer book]?" The offering of this simple boy ascended before the throne of the Almighty and was given priority over all other prayers. The story was meant to emphasize the power of innocent prayer — especially when it comes from the hearts of children — before the Almighty. And so she prayed on in silence, shedding many tears, hoping that her plea for safety will be granted.

It was late at night when the grandmother opened the closet door, liberating her and offering some nourishment. They had come searching through the house, she was told, in one of their routine inspections of Jewish dwellings. They looked everywhere, but didn't detect the closet door!

"Thank God, you escaped!" was the way her grandparents put it. Yes, she escaped! The protective hand that has been guiding her footsteps was still spread over her, still shielding her! She murmurs a few words of thanksgiving and falls asleep with a heart filled with gratitude....

It is early in the evening on a late summer's day. She is sitting in her bedroom, waiting. The house is quiet, and gloomy. The windows are closed and the shades, as always, are drawn. She has just finished preparing, said good night and is trying to read for a while, but is restless — she cannot concentrate.

She gets up and walks to the window. She raises a corner of the shade and takes a peek. Outside it is not yet dark. She can make out the tiny stream deep down in the ravine, winding its way to the Downs. The sky is deep and darkening — a mixture of gray, purple and red hues, with streaks of light near the horizon in the wake of the setting sun. She can still see the trees, shrubs and flowers along the expanse of the ravine, which will soon disappear into the darkness of the night.

Is she really going to chance it? It will be a frightening experience, she knows that, but wonderful if she succeeds. It will be a change, a bit of a break in her routine. She has befriended the daughter of the local schochet, a girl by the name of Rechi, somewhat older, but in the same position she is in: illegal in her own house. The grandfather had called a meeting recently and Rechi's parents brought her along.

"The girl is taking unnecessary chances!" the grandfather observed after they left, and the grandmother nodded in assent. The significance of the exchange wasn't lost on Sheinda: she mustn't get any ideas....

"But now, ironically, she is to take chances herself; she is to go to Rechi's house for a while, until it becomes less risky here with her grandparents.

Rechi's parents had been consulted and Rechi had given her precise directions about the way she is to proceed; the way she is to make her way along the ravine. Under cover of darkness, late at night, there would be no one there to observe her...it would be safe. Once there, she will inform the grandparents that she is safe and will wait for their instructions.

"It is actually a neat plan," she thinks, "I need a break...oh, how I need it. What a great adventure this would be if not for the fear."

She waits until it is pitch dark, then quietly makes her way into the yard. She creeps along the wall of the house until the very bottom of the courtyard and onto the footpath leading down the steep ravine. When she reaches the bottom she turns left and carefully makes her way along the bank of the creek toward the Downs, whence it will be only a short way to her friend's house.

Her progress is slow, for it is dark and it takes her a while before she is able to discern the objects in her path. She uses her hands — reaching out and around her...groping in the manner of the blind. She cannot afford to stumble or fall; an accident here would be a tragedy....

After a while her eyes become accustomed to the conditions and she is able to make out the tree stumps, shrubs and other matter. The path is strewn with twigs and leaves that rustle underneath her feet. She tries to tiptoe over them so as to minimize the noise. She must be careful to avoid stumbling over the stones, as well.

Glad as she is to be alone, unobserved, she finds the journey desolate — frightening really. The night air is cold and damp; there is moisture on the ground — probably dew, mixed with a bit of early frost. She shivers — should have taken her overcoat, but it is too late now...she must hurry! Her overcoat, moreover, would be little protection against tremors caused by her fear.... No matter, she should soon reach her destination. Time to consider her approach to the house and the signal she is to give her friend when she gets there. She must avoid waking her parents!

She decides to approach the house through the back. Rechi's bedroom is above the kitchen, she was told, its window a few feet above where she is now standing. The small ladder she will need is underneath the tree to her right. She moves the ladder to the wall underneath the window, climbs to the top and knocks on the glass three time, their pre-arranged signal.

She waits, but hears no movement in the room. Rechi appears to be soundly asleep, even though it is not late, probably just barely past midnight. She decides to knock again, this time putting a bit of energy into the motion. She hears a stirring inside and soon Rechi is at the window having realized, with a start, what is going on. The window is now open and Rechi whispers to her to climb in carefully. This she does with great haste, having at last completed her arduous and lonely undertaking.

"You're here, at last!" Rechi exclaims, but checks herself immediately and resumes her whispering mode. They don't want to waken the parents; they want the entire night to themselves!

"How did it go?" Rechi inquires; "Was it very difficult?"

"No, just a bit lonely and cold. I did have to get used to moving in the dark. And I was afraid, of course. Not so much of people, as of some animal. You never know what may cross your path in the night!"

"I'm so glad you're here in one piece — and nothing happened! I would feel terrible if something bad happened to you. Well, no need to worry about that now."

"Yes, I know. But I'm so glad to be here — I want to thank you, dear, for making it possible — you saved me from dying of boredom too!"

"Great, make yourself comfortable, won't you? I think these will fit you," Rechi says, handing her a pair of old flannel pajamas she pulls from her closet.

Sheinda undresses and slips into the warm pajamas, then sits on the edge of the bed and waits for her friend who soon returns with a tray of cookies and milk. They sit on the bed, the tray between them, consuming the food, then settle down on the floor in one corner of the room to talk.

Rechi speaks of her family's plan to avoid deportation. They are to cross the border, she is saying, into the territory of the neighboring state, only a short distance from their town. But not yet. For the time being it is safe here. The two of them may find the time to become good friends during the interval.

Yes, that would be nice; she hopes so too. Her own family has a similar plan, she knows, in case they needed to run...but she doesn't want to talk about it. No, there will be plenty of time to inform her friend. Right now she must give herself totally to the exhilaration of this adventure! Here they are, the two of them, in this nocturnal meeting...after her successful escape from her house. She had endured fear, and trepidation; ran with her heart in her mouth, so to speak, the entire journey, but all of it had held a degree of excitement...yes, even her fear! Now, in the calm of this cozy room, in the company of the girl facing her, she feels calm: reassured, all of her recent anxiety gone. She is observing Rechi, who now sits quietly absorbed in her own thought.

Rechi is thin and tall. She has dark brown, wavy hair parted in the middle and combed back behind her ears. Her dark blue eyes seem larger than they are, perhaps because her face is long and narrow. Her thin but pleasantly outlined lips are soft, and at the moment, are turned up in an absent smile. She is well formed: with narrow hips and pretty legs, though a bit flat-chested. The overall image, though, is attractive.

"Rechi is old; she must be at least eighteen, perhaps more," Sheinda reflects. Probably too old for them to have ever become friends, given normal circumstances. But in her present situation Rechi is a Godsend...and so kind; such a pleasant creature. Rechi's sweetness is the trait that makes itself most felt — her outstanding characteristic. Yes, she will enjoy this visit and has reason to look forward to a lasting friendship with this fine girl.

"Would you like to play some game?" Rechi asks, interrupting their silence.

"Yes, for a while, sure!" she replies. Her friend brings over a box of dominoes and they throw themselves into play as if nothing else mattered. Sheinda wins and is elated by her victory. Rechi takes the pieces apart, carries away the game and they each take their place on opposite sides of the narrow bed. Soon she hears the soft, measured breathing of her new friend and after saying a hurried prayer, she turns toward the wall and sleeps.

In the morning Rechi wakes her. She had slept the sleep of a tired child, and is now facing her friend's parents, who are already in possession of the details of her night's adventure.

She is surprised by their hospitality and their wonderful sense of humor. There is something very different about them. What is it? What makes them stand out so? She thinks about it and decides that it's their extraordinary kindness; they're humble, self-effacing, as though they had nothing in the world to attend to that is more important than making her comfortable. No wonder...this is where Rechi takes her attitude from! What a great family this is...she feels elated, thankful that such people exist still, and that she has the good fortune to have crossed their path.

Her grandparents are informed that all is well and agree to extend her visit for a few extra days. She spends an entire week with her friend and her family, participates in all their activities as though she were one of them and, basking in their loving kindness, is able to forget all of her worries and anxieties. She will not soon forget the experience!

Two weeks later she is back home, immersed in the old routines. She is glad that the grandparents had agreed to extend her visit and is very careful to show her gratitude. They, on their part, are equally anxious to please her; she is touched to see them going out of their way to show that they care.

The grandmother opens the great cupboard in the vestibule which, in the olden days, had always been locked. She reaches in and removes a few crumbly cup cakes, offering them to her granddaughter in her most generous gesture. Sheinda takes one and attempts a bite, but stops with the thing in mid air. A strong, moldy odor emanates from the cake and she reluctantly puts it on an empty plate on the table. "I will eat it later," she explains, wishing to spare the grandmother.

The grandfather is also showing thoughtfulness. She still sees him rushing around or pacing his study in nervous agitation — his forehead furrowed, his face flushed — intent upon some urgent matter having to do with their safety and oblivious to all else. But he makes it his business now, more than ever before, to seek her out; to offer a smile, a jest, or a word of encouragement. He does this in his inimitable manner, with deliberation, courtliness and charm. It is his way of letting her know that she matters and she humbly accepts his gift of grace. It is the beginning of their reconciliation.

She is taking chances now. Evenings, when all around seems quiet, she sometimes slips out into the yard and walks down the slope toward the outhouse. In the beginning of that venture she would slip into the grandmother's clothes: with a shawl thrown over her shoulders and a kerchief tied under her chin in the manner of the old lady, her disguise wasn't bad. Oh, she didn't expect to fool anyone up close, but some unsuspecting neighbor catching sight of her thus walking down the path, would take it for granted that it is the grandmother.

Lately, she no longer bothered with the disguise. It meant delay...and she was eager to leave the house. The opportunity to visit with her friend Rechi was no longer there. She had repeated the visit once, and her friend had come to stay with her for a few days. But there came the day when Rechi informed her that she is leaving town, and now she is gone! Her evening walks in the courtyard, prolonged by a lengthy stay in the outhouse, have become a necessity to her. She craves not only diversion from her confinement in the house, but also a bit of outdoor air. She has worked out a system by now: she walks around in the yard for a bit, then runs for cover — even when no one appears on the scene, just as a matter of precaution — then she repeats the procedure alternating between walks in the yard and sessions in the outhouse. She has a stack of reading material, which she keeps, in a paper bag in a corner by the door. Under the bag she has a folded old blanket which she uses to cover the hole in the seat — thereby eliminating somewhat the unpleasant privy odor, while at the same time adding comfort to the hard, wooden seat. Confinement in the outhouse is the price she must, and is quite willing, to pay for the pleasure of walking in the yard whenever her fancy strikes her.

Of late she has even begun running into the yard during the daytime, whenever her need arises, and that's what she is doing on this sunny fall afternoon. She lingers in the yard for a bit, inhaling the pungent scent of the drying grass and falling leaves, allowing the vanishing rays of the sun to stroke her. She looks across the fence into the widow's garden and contemplates a surprise visit to her house.

"That would be nice," she thinks, and is sorely tempted, but decides against it at the last moment. "No, I better get going," she thinks, "I don't want to overdo it," and she slowly makes her way toward the house.

She is walking slowly and is practically within reach of the front door when the gate leading to the street is suddenly thrown open. At the very same moment she slides toward the wall of the house and slips into the doorway to one of the lower apartments.

She manages to peer out from under the door that conceals her and sees a large contingent of the local police and gendarmerie enter the yard. They rap on the front door requesting entry amid much angry shouting and boisterous laughter. Sheinda remains there — hidden from view — until the last man appears to have entered the house. She slowly opens the door, peeks out and, realizing that the coast is clear, runs to her outhouse hideaway and closes the door.

She utilizes the first few moments to compose herself. She sits on the wooden board of the privy, huddling against the wall in one of its corners. She must first bring her trembling under control. Once this is accomplished, she will be able to think...perhaps to discern the meaning of this latest threat! She manages to stop her trembling, but her heart is still beating wildly. She tries to sit quietly, without moving, and tells herself that she is probably safe — at least for the time being. It isn't likely that anyone saw her. If they had, she reasons, they would have been after her long before now. The question, now, is whether they will be looking here, in the outhouse...and whether or not they do so depends on what they are here for! The best she can do is hope and pray that Providence will once again save her; allow her to remain with her loved ones.

She summons up her courage, removes the blanket from underneath the bag, places it over the privy hole, takes a book out of the bag, sits down and begins to read. This will be the best way, she knows, to keep calm and wait.

But she cannot do it, she can't read! The danger is too close...! She becomes restless, cannot concentrate. She closes her eyes — "perhaps this will calm my nerves," she thinks and sits quietly for a while. Her head begins to ache and she strokes her temples absentmindedly in the attempt to ease the pain, while reviewing her new predicament:

"What will happen to me?" she reflects..."what if they are actually searching for me? Someone must have seen me and informed...! It's only a matter of time before they find me here and send me away! Dear God," she prays, (aware though she is that the privy is unsuitable for prayer) "don't let it happen! Please, please save me from the horror of being dragged away alone...!" She moves to the corner of the seat, near the wall and closes her eyes again. "I will try to sleep," she thinks, but she is cold. She gets up, removes the blanket she sits on and wraps it around herself — then sits down again, pressing herself snugly into the corner of two adjoining walls.

Outside it is dark...night has descended! She listens to the sounds around her...hoping to hear scraping of boots on the cobblestones, boisterous shouts or some other signs of departure, but she hears nothing, not a sound from the direction of the house. All she hears is the nocturnal noise of the crickets and frogs — from around the creek at the bottom of the ravine. She is accustomed to that sound, is reassured by it. It brings with it the illusion of the ordinary, the usual, the normal. She closes her eyes once more pretending, this time, to be in her bed with her window wide open, listening to the night sound around her, as she so often does. She is soon asleep.

She escaped once again! It was almost noon of the next day, by the time she finally ventures forth from her hiding place. The grandparents had been frantic when, following the departure of the police, they had discovered her absence from her room — fearing that she had somehow fallen victim...during the confusion of events. — But the search had not been about her! No, there had been no need for an extensive search of the premises. It had been another one of the routine checks of the Jewish dwellings — to appease the radical elements within the local government who demanded continued persecution. But, how lucky for her that she had momentarily been away from the house! How lucky indeed. They may not have been looking for her, but what if they had found her? Had she been there, in the house, there would have been no excuse for them...they would have had to take her, to save their own skins! She was overwhelmed with astonishment and awe — someone, up there, was truly watching over her....

Among the remaining families in town were the Fellers — a corpulent couple very dedicated to each other. They were among those able to buy their freedom...those who returned home at the very last moment....

He, a man in his middle forties, was clean-shaven with a round face and ruddy complexion. Short, with a protruding belly, he was outwardly easygoing, but a tough businessman, known to drive a hard bargain. She, an obese matron with a double chin, was constantly smiling and very sweet when it pleased her, but inaccessible to those whose favor she didn't curry.

Sheinda saw them occasionally. The husband was now in charge of some of the communal responsibilities. Whenever he had business to conduct with the grandfather, his wife would accompany him and chat with the grandmother in the girl's presence.

The girl enjoyed these rare visits. Mrs. Feller was well informed — she was in command of all that went on in town; knew what was cooking in every pot and her little vignettes could be amusing. Much of her small talk consisted of gossip, including all manner of petty complaining and backbiting.

Sheinda found it startling at first. Didn't the woman have anything serious to be concerned about? But she got used to the day-to-day trivial concerns of Mrs. Feller, no matter how unsavory, and came to look forward to her visits. The very pettiness of the woman proved distracting; it helped bring back something of the aura of "normalcy" to her daily routine.

She also admired the woman's ability to keep her husband's unstinting affection and support. No matter how biting Mrs. Feller's comments, her husband stood by her to praise, cheer, or applaud. In his eyes she was the perfect woman! She must have done something right, the girl reasoned, to be the recipient of such deep affection. The phenomenon taught her something of the complexity of human nature — how one must not judge people lightly.

CHAPTER SEVEN
ESCAPE

Then one day it came to pass. Late one night, as prearranged, an individual appeared at the gate and was admitted into the house. He surveyed briefly the packages they had prepared and instructed them to unpack it all and place everything on the table. He then proceeded to reduce the lot by half and divided what remained into three small bundles. They each took hold of one — and filed out in silence behind the man who was to be their guide toward and across the border.

They trudged on in silence; in the darkest of nights without the benefit of moonlight to lighten their path, all of it by design. It was dark, cold and wearisome. They walked on for hours without rest — mostly through field and forest — until toward dawn they finally reached the first stop of their journey, the village that lay on the border.

Their guide took them into a peasant hut where several other families were assembled. They had all come from different localities, but were headed toward the same destination — the large city directly across the border. The guide distributed blankets; they each got one and he instructed them to get as much rest as possible during the daytime hours.

Get some rest? Easier said than done! They were in a room with bare walls and a cold dirt floor. How were they going to rest here? They could lie on the blanket or cover themselves with it — not both. Nevertheless, their fatigue compelled them to try.

The grandmother folded her blanket in two and placed it on the ground in a corner of the room. She helped the girl onto the "bed," lay down beside her, then used the second blanket to cover them both. The girl, closest to the wall, turned toward it and closed her eyes.

She tried to sleep but couldn't — distracted by the turmoil of a village at work; by the hum of voices around her as well as by inner anxiety.

Once again she is running without knowing exactly where she will wind up — or whether she will succeed in getting there. True, she is not alone this time. She is with the grandparents and hopefully she will manage to remain with them. But their prospects are so unclear, so uncertain; nothing is predictable!

She is awake now; must have slept some after all, and they are given some bread and milk by the guide and other members of his family who assist him. Outside it is getting dark and their guide is collecting his fees for taking them across the border from each party. He is also attempting to provide them with instructions for this most dangerous leg of their journey.

It isn't clear to Sheinda what the provisions he has made are: has he actually managed to bribe the border patrol, or is he trying to evade them? She guesses the latter to be the case, because his emphasis is on utmost discretion and care. There is to be no conversation for the entire stretch of the crossing. They are to go single file, treading as lightly as possible to avoid all rustling and noise. They are responsible each for their own bundle — there is to be no assistance.

When the time comes they all pick up their packs and file out behind the individual who is to take them across. It turns out that there has been a last minute substitution. The man they are following is not the individual who had brought them thus far. Their guide now is a tall, awkward lad — a mere youth devoid of authority — who doesn't inspire much confidence. He appears to have been pressed into service by his willingness to please his elders; by their demand, rather than by his suitability for the task. He does seem to have had prior experience, however. They aren't the first group he is leading across, they are told.

They aren't protesting. There is no time to do so, nor do they have any choice in the matter. His youth, his lack of experience and confidence do not matter in the end. After all, says one old woman, "az Got wil, sheest a bezem [if God wills it a broom can shoot]." Perhaps, they reason, this young fellow was chosen to be the instrument of leading them to freedom. Who knows? Perhaps he did something to merit the distinction of being their savior. And if it be so, what does it matter how old he is, how much experience he has, or how much confidence he inspires? So they follow him without complaint.

The night is damp and cold; once again there is no moon. The twenty some people in the group trudge on, slowly making their way over hill and dale with difficulty and caution. But the dark sky is clear without any clouds and no rain is expected.

"Good night for a crossing," says the young fellow unexpectedly.

"All you need now is a bit of luck!" he continues, perhaps in the attempt to raise their fallen spirits.

"I think you will bring us the luck we need," says the old lady — the one given to Yiddish adages.

"Omein" [Amen], echo the rest and they walk on with a bit more zest.

They have been walking for what seems like hours and are within sight of a clearing where they expect to take a rest. They have covered about half the distance they need to go when suddenly, from afar, they hear the unmistakable sound of barking dogs. They must be close to a settlement — some outlying farm between villages — and have alerted the dogs watching for intruders; or might have stumbled across the border patrol!

Their guide motions to them to stop where they are. He sits down on the damp ground that is covered with a thick layer of needles from a variety of pine and spruce, mixed with heaps of leaves and other debris. They all sink down exhausted, huddling around him, trying to control their fear. He doesn't speak, but motions to them to remain in their positions. His gestures suggest that he is waiting for the barking to cease; they must wait, sit immobilized, before they can resume their walk.

Sheinda sits petrified with fear. She hadn't realized until that very moment all of the possible dangers threatening them. Of course, she knew — she did understand in a superficial way — that dangers lurked behind every turn, but only now does her fear begin to manifest itself physically. She begins to tremble — her entire body literally shaking with fear — and she is unable to control it; is totally incapacitated by it, her body convulsed by tremors.

She tries to hide her discomfort and embarrassment over her inability to bring it under control. She sits with her head between her knees so as not to have to look at anyone and presses herself as close to the ground as she can manage — as if wishing to sink into it.

The guide, only a few paces away, couldn't help noticing but gives no sign — he ignores it all. He sits quietly, as do the rest of them, until the barking slowly subsides, then altogether ceases. Only then does he rise to his feet slowly and gives the sign for the rest of them to follow suit. He is taking a slightly changed direction, a roundabout way to the resting ground, in order to put some distance between them and those dogs.

The group, very cautiously now, commences the journey. They move slowly, without noise, in the direction indicated.
After a while the guide approaches the girl who is near the end of the line. He falls in behind her and places a hand on her shoulder.

"Are you all right?" he inquires in a barely audible whisper.

"Yes, thank you. I'm okay."

"I think I will help you carry this," he says removing the bag from her back. "You seem fine now, but you were shivering back there. You ought to hold on to me; It'll help you get warm," he says and takes her hand. "We must stop that trembling. You mustn't get sick on us now...!"

He walks on quietly holding her hand; she is uncomfortable, fidgets, thinking of a way to free herself tactfully. After a while he puts his arm around her hugging her in a matter-of-fact manner. The girl is disturbed. She knows she mustn't allow anyone of the opposite sex to get close, to hold and caress her. It's forbidden, she must stop that. At the same time there is no denying the steadying effect of his action. Her body has responded to the warmth of his proximity and the soothing of his hands. She stopped trembling, feels reassured — no longer overwhelmed by fear. However, her discomfort lingers.

"I know you want to help me" she finally gets up her courage to say as she withdraws her hand, "but you mustn't do this, it's against our rules. I will be punished, don't you see?"

"Will you? Why?" He turns his gaze upon her in candid scrutiny as if wishing to know more. She looks up at him in silence saying no more. But her eyes — have they spoken for her as he held them just now? What, besides fear, did he see in them? Loneliness? Hunger? Need for the human touch? Did he detect yearnings she wouldn't recognize or comprehend?

He touches her hand lightly saying only "I understand," the bare shadow of a smile flitting across his face. They speak no more and resume their walk — she falling in behind the others; he making his way to the top of the line.

They walk on for a short while and soon reach their destination: the shelter in the forest — a neglected campground with tents scattered among the trees and a wooden structure in the middle of a clearing — where they are to rest. It is a small structure built of wood — sort of a cabin, of what appears to be an abandoned camp. About half of the group find accommodation within, the rest find shelter in the tents under nearby trees. After a short meal of bread and cheese, which they had carried with them, they all repair to their designated corner to get some sleep.

Sheinda takes leave of her grandparents and walks toward the tent assigned to her. She looks around her, but can see little. It is still pitch dark — the day has not yet dawned; whatever might be visible of the horizon, unobscured by the trees, remains hidden by the night. The forest is still, its nocturnal repose rent periodically by the hooting of an owl and the sounds of other night creatures. She quickens her pace conscious of her total isolation in this lonely stillness of the night. She walks on, soon reaching the tent pointed out to her and is looking forward to her rest.

She enters quietly so as not to disturb anyone, but to her surprise the tent is empty. She is taken aback, disappointed, but soon rallies to her task. She removes one of the two folded blankets she finds on the floor, spreads it out in one corner of the tent and lies down. She stretches to her full length then curls up, pulling one side of the blanket over her body to serve her as a cover. She needs to get some sleep.

She must have slept some, but is awake now conscious of the sound of steady, measured breathing coming from the other side of the tent. She sits up slowly and looks across, curious about the identity of the individual sleeping on the other side. She discovers, to her astonishment, that it is the young peasant, their guide.

"My God! Why? Why is he here?" Frightened, she puts this question to herself, but realizes the futility of her puzzlement. It doesn't matter why, does it? The fact is he is here and she must remove herself immediately. Yes! She shall go at once! She slips on her shoes and very quietly without any audible sound moves forward ready to make her exit. She has reached the tent partition that serves as the door and is about to make her escape when his voice, clear and strong, stops her in her tracks.

"Where do you think you are going?" he asks calmly. "You better come back here! I want to talk to you before you go!"

His matter-of-fact demeanor is reassuring.

"Control yourself, you little idiot," she argues with herself. "It's obvious the fellow means no harm! You better do as you're told!"

She turns around and walks toward him stopping midway between the door and his "lodging" just as he is getting up.

He sits on his blanket slipping on his shoes then rises to his full height and moves to meet her. He is very tall and she is tiny — he must bend down to talk to her and does so now.

"Were you able to get some sleep?" he asks.

"Yes, I think so, I feel rested. I must have slept and didn't hear you come in, but I think I should leave now."

"Yes, of course. You didn't expect me here, did you? I didn't mean to startle you. You should not be here alone." He turns away from her, as if to go back to his bed, then changes course unexpectedly.

"Let me feel your hands," he says suddenly and takes her hands in his. "I must make sure you're no longer cold — as you were then, remember?" He smiles, holding her close again.

His action overwhelms her, rooting her to the spot.

"No, you seem fine now, but I want to make sure you stay that way," he says and pulls her down beside him.

"I can make you real warm," he continues and swings his long frame over her small body, supporting himself on his elbows as he looks down at her, then lowers his torso with only his head slightly raised. He has her on her back, pinned down, barely able to move and frightened beyond words.

"My God!" she thinks, "what is happening to me? What is he going to do to me now?" Her heart is pounding wildly but she is trying to control her fear. She feels that she mustn't panic, mustn't alienate him — that her only chance is to convince him to let her go.

"Have you ever been kissed?" he says, covering her mouth with his lips that linger over hers, then move to her face, neck and shoulders.

"No, I don't think you have, have you? I think I must give you a lesson now. Would you like to learn about love? I will be gentle," he whispers, "I won't hurt you, you'll see. I've had lots of practice."

His body is pressed close to hers; she can feel a bulge — hard, with a tip like steel — pressing itself against her. A wave of warmth unexpectedly sweet suffuses her body. She can feel herself relax — her resistance threatening to give way under his pressure and this new sensation. She is in danger of surrender, but recovers her will at the very last moment. She knows she mustn't let this happen! — she must speak now, there is no time to waste. She frees one of her hands and raising herself to face him says quietly:

"I know you mean no harm! I have seen fellows back home with girls from the village; they all do this and no one seems to mind. But it's different for me! I am not allowed, it's against our rules! Do let me go, please!" She turns her frightened eyes, filled now with a silent plea, towards him. "Please, I must leave now!"

"Must you? — I only wanted to love you: make you feel good!" He speaks softly as if in defense of his action with suddenly a helpless, forlorn air about him. "Okay, okay, I won't!" he reassures, seeing her tears. "But can I just hold you — make sure you're all right?" he says this as if prompted by a need to save face.

Relieved, she stops protesting. She relaxes, aware that the danger is past. She can afford to humor him now — play along with him. Gradually her sense of outrage gives way and a feeling of gratitude fills her. She is grateful for his understanding; for his willingness to put her need before his own.

As he lets her go, she says "Thank you!" This is all she manages to say. She wants to say more — express her overwhelming sense of relief — but is unable to do it. She steps away from him and makes her way to the door.

"Thank you," she whispers again and leaves to make her way to the main compound.

Only much later does she comprehend fully the import of his deed. He wanted to give her a lesson in love, and he did. He had shown her that he cared — that such people, strangers who cared, still existed.

The rest of their journey followed a similar pattern; they rested by day and walked by night. The road seemed interminable — as though it might never end. They trudged through forest and meadow and through brooks and mud up to their knees.

At times they were forced into unscheduled stops — as during a fierce thunderstorm when they sat under a tree and waited until the forest was calm again, or when danger from nearby settlements threatened — following one of which they had to run and throw away all their "excess" baggage. But one night their journey did come to an end. They finally arrived in the city on the other side of the border — the city into which they were headed. Her great-grandfather who had lived here for years, had passed on some years ago and left his widow and young son behind. They still lived here in the house she knew so well, having spent many a pleasant vacation there during her childhood.

The grandparents were stationed with a prominent local family, but she stayed with her "aunt" as the great-grandfather's widow was referred to by family members.

Sheinda found the house much the same as of old, but the household had been reduced: gone were the cook, the maids and the manservant, leaving only Leah, the housekeeper, to take care of the daily chores. It was Leah also who now loyally supplemented the family income by sewing women's underwear and selling it to local stores. A daughter could have done no more!

Leah is petite and mousy looking with short dark hair that is never quite in place. Her nose is prominent and her teeth are uneven and somewhat discolored, giving her an impish look when she smiles. She uses makeup improperly, applying it a bit heavily — without much foundation — to her dry skin. The result is unbecoming.

But the girl is unaware of Leah's blemishes. Were she to be asked for her candidate to win the local beauty contest, her choice may well be Leah. For Leah's inner beauty shines out of her being, drowning out all other impressions. Yes, Leah is beautiful: her goodness, love and self-sacrifice are enough to cover all her bodily faults.

Leah is also mature and very competent. She came into service to the family as a young girl to assist with the housekeeping chores. As the years went by she took over as chief housekeeper.

Later, as the staff was being reduced, she took on all other functions. At present she not only runs the house, but is a loyal companion and breadwinner as well. In their present reduced circumstances, the family would be unable to make ends meet without the loyal support of Leah.

Sheinda likes being in the house of her great aunt. She enjoys playing with the boy, (the great-grandfather fathered a child in his seventies) and fondly recalls the many excursions and shopping trips into town with "Aunt", who understands children and has always made it her business to delight her in some special way. But most of all, Sheinda enjoys watching Leah, who takes her under her wing.

There are other diversions for her in this town: an uncle, her father's brother and his young family live here as well — and so does the family Gross whose many children she counts among her closest childhood friends. On one visit to the house of the latter, which had to be undertaken at night at great discretion, she is surprised by the visit of their son Motty, their oldest child.

Motty, her frequent companion on her childhood visits to the city. How fond she had been of him, how exciting their games and activities. He liked to have her about and she followed him like a little dog. He found time to teach her things: older than she by several years and ahead of her in school, they shared the same scholastic background and atmosphere. He was familiar with the books she read, the projects she was involved in and was able to anticipate and appreciate her work. Sometimes he would assist her with an idea, or task. But the best part was his identification with her efforts. He shared her goals, as it were, and that gave her confidence.

Sometimes they would chase through yards and meadows, then sit quietly side by side enjoying their rest. He also liked to pick her up and carry her around on his shoulders when she got tired. The thing she remembers best, however, was his ready laugh: a ringing infectious laugh that brought much joy to them both.

She grew excited when told that he was at home visiting, curious of the change the years had wrought.

"Let me see, it must be at least five years, isn't it, since I last saw him?" she said to herself. "Yes, at least five years! That's a long time! He probably no longer remembers me! It will never be the same again."

The thought barely managed to flash across her consciousness when there is a sudden rap on the door.

"Come in!" she calls out and waits for the door to open.

She had been taken up to the attic, the only real safe place in the apartment, Mrs. Gross had pointed out — away from snooping neighbors! So here she was, alone, when the others were occupied with their daily routine.

The door creaks open and in walks a strange young man in what looks like an Army uniform.

"Is this Motty? — Yes," she reflects and moves forward closing the distance between them. He, too, is moving to meet her and stops awkwardly a few paces away. She looks at him attentively. Motty! He looks older, with the mature and serious air of an adult about him. She can also detect traces of sadness and pain around his eyes and mouth, as if branded by some recent experience. But the change is subtle, not all that obvious. He seems shorter, but with the same pleasant cheerful face, wide mouth, large blue eyes and blond head, just as she remembers him. His manner, now, is reserved and somewhat distant, as though he had things on his mind weighing him down. He speaks at last:

"You're looking at my clothes, aren't you? I wear this uniform because I'm on leave from my base, which is not far away. I was lucky to be able to get a few days off. I don't know when I'll be home again."

"Are you a soldier, then? I thought they had guns, but I see you don't have one, do you?"

"No, you're right, I don't! I belong to the work brigades, which accompany the armed force. We do the work, the digging of ditches and other very difficult jobs. We are issued shovels, not guns. We are mostly Jews, and are doing the punitive work. I could tell you some stories, some gruesome things I've witnessed, but I would rather spare you! Why worry about things you don't need to know? I haven't told my folks all I know either."

"It's good to see you," he moves closer and touches her shoulder lightly, then quickly removes his hand.

"I've heard what you have gone through and I'm in a position to believe what I hear. As I said, I've seen a lot myself...It seems as though the carefree times we — I mean you and I — have known; the times of our childhood — they are gone for good, never to return."

81

"Yes, how true!" she brings out softly.

"I've had some dreams of my own, personal dreams, which are shattered now. We are to be shipped to the East soon, very soon. Who knows when I shall return?"

"Dreams of his own? Personal dreams? What is he talking about?" she wonders, then stops, as the thought dawns on her. "Of course, how stupid I am! He has a sweetheart, is probably engaged to be married, in love with someone." A stab of jealousy flashes through her; she cannot help feeling disappointed, as though something she has long known to be hers is suddenly removed from her.

She makes an effort to say something; some words that would express her hopes for his plans and good fortune, but she cannot! She struggles to give voice to some words she has formed, but nothing comes out of her mouth — she remains standing in silence.

"I will have to be leaving soon," he says, interrupting her thoughts.

"Oh, you mean back to your base?" she asks, the brevity of his visit suddenly very tangible for her.

"Yes. I know some of my buddies won't be returning. They have chosen to desert; to go into hiding, but I have no stomach for that. I will take my chances hoping for the best. This war cannot go on forever."

"He is hopeful," she muses, like the people she had overheard as they were being led from their homes to the synagogue:

"The enemy are sure to lose the war!" they had argued; "the Russians are stopping them and we shall soon return home!" But setbacks at the front didn't reverse the decrees, didn't stop the persecution at home nor in the concentration camps. Now Motty, too, will be at their mercy!

"I wish I could stay a while longer, but I must go now — take care!" He says these words with a smile, then turns towards the door and is gone.

The Grosses live under reduced circumstances; have been living this way for years. Mr. Gross, a thin man of medium height with red hair and a fair complexion had abandoned his failing business many years ago and went off to America there to seek a better fortune. From there he sent glowing letters to his family at home: about the opportunities...the fortunes to be had in the "golden land." After he returned — for return he did — he couldn't stop talking about his experiences. He promised to go back one day, this time with his family, and was known among his friends and acquaintances as "the American." But of course that hope, along with other dreams, vanished long ago and the family remained at home.

Every morning Mr. Gross would go through the routine of a man preparing to go to work. He would carefully select his clothes from his meager wardrobe and make certain that his suit, coat and hat were immaculate. His shoes, likewise, shone like a mirror. After all, he was on his way to a day's work — wasn't he? Yes, indeed! He would faithfully leave his house for work each morning, but where exactly he went and what he did there no one knew for certain....

Some believed that he went to look for employment...others that he hustled around the local stock exchange where he allegedly had several irons in the fire. Somehow, these many deals always petered out just as they were about to be closed and Mr. Gross was left holding the empty bag....

But setbacks in business don't seem to discourage Mr. Gross. No matter how agonizing his day, and today is an example, he comes home in a jolly mood — as though he had just "struck it rich," and announces his arrival as soon as he crosses the threshold.

"Well, hello...hello! I'm home, everyone! Come out and greet your father, children!" he yells from the doorway then hurries to meet his oncoming flock. He is soon surrounded and disappears in a sea of arms, legs and bobbing little heads — amid enthusiastic shouts of welcome that drown out his own words and laughter. He allows his children to detain him clowning around with them for a while, then turns to greet his wife:

"Mama, my dear, how was your day?"

"Thank you, my breadwinner, and how was yours?" retorts Mrs. Gross, a stout, full-blown woman with blue eyes and a blond peruke — her broad, pleasant face distorted momentarily by a sarcastic frown:

"I dare say you did it today! You finally did nail down our fortune, right?" She comes closer, examines his face and continues: "You mean you didn't? Oh, no! Not again!" she exclaims in mock astonishment, her smile and manner betraying mild scorn and resignation at his repeated failure.

"That's too bad...isn't it? Well, come on in and have some supper...tomorrow will be another day!"

Mr. Gross appears to take his wife's remarks in stride and follows her sheepishly into the large, bare kitchen in the middle of which stands a table set for the evening meal. The parents and their children take their seats around it,

Dinner today consists of a hot tomato soup into which green peppers, stuffed with a mixture of rice and chopped meat have been lowered and allowed to simmer for about two hours. Plenty of sugar and salt and pepper to taste rendered it into a tasty and nourishing dish.

Sheinda, their guest from the attic, is being welcomed and heartily encouraged to join in their feast which they all engage in with great zest. She is hungry and is grateful for their hospitality. She enjoys the food, which is quite good. She cleans her plate and would like some more, but is aware that there is barely enough for one serving to each participant.

Nevertheless, Mrs. Gross reaches for her plate and returns it with another generous portion. Her own children fare less well: they hungrily follow their mother's action but remain silent. One determined look from her is sufficient to still their unuttered plea. They understand, there simply isn't enough for seconds...!

One exception is Maidy, their youngest child, for whom they all go out of their way, bringing her their best morsels. She is an enchanting little girl of five with a head of golden curls, big blue eyes and radiant smile who delights with her talk and laughter. Only lately she isn't laughing. For some time now Maidy has been ill — something in the bone of her right leg — and she sits in her wheelchair seeing all but saying little.

The young girl has other acquaintances and family to visit and spend time with here, among them her Uncle Chaimel, his wife and children. Uncle Chaimel is a short, wiry man with a thin, blond beard. He moves about with energy and speed and gives off an aura of competence. On her visits to their apartment — they live in a modern high-rise structure with central heating and water that comes out of the wall — he has been very solicitous, very kind to her. She was puzzled by his attitude at first, but has gotten accustomed to it. It is the manner one exhibits toward an orphan.

His wife, Aunt Dena, is a fine-looking woman. A head taller than her husband, she carries herself with dignity and grace. Her attire is dark and she wears a headdress similar to that of Sheinda's mother. Aunt Dena has regular, classic features presided over by beautiful brown eyes. She is a well liked individual; her husband, Uncle Chaimel, being a great admirer of hers.

The couple has two daughters. The older, Freidele, is a pretty youngster of about ten, with blond braids dangling from her shoulders. She has her mother's self-confidence and poise, is outgoing and articulate; wants to know the meaning of things, of the upheavals that brought her cousin to town.

Her little sister Rachele is about seven. She resembles her father in stature and in looks and, though bright and pleasant, is somewhat withdrawn. They all go out of their way to make their cousin welcome. Perhaps there was some news from the East... perhaps they know something and aren't telling her? She doesn't know what it is, exactly...she only senses a difference in their attitude — something...that wasn't there before!

She remains only a short while with her uncle's family. The remaining week in this city she spends with the family Brown. Mr. Brown is a prosperous merchant in town. He and his wife, well-dressed and dignified individuals, live in a beautiful house. They have a married daughter in the capital city and two young girls at home.

The elder of the two is a dark beauty who has been out of school for a while. She must be at least eighteen years old. Tall and slim with thick wavy dark hair and lovely black eyes, she has a statuesque, regal presence. The other girl, a good deal younger, is still in school. She is in a growing, transitional stage; it is difficult to predict what she will turn into.

Sheinda admires them, their environment, their circle of friends — largely imaginary, for she doesn't meet their friends — and secretly imagines herself to be part of their set, but she is aware that she doesn't and probably never will belong....

She listens to their talk in bed at night and hears that Chava, the older girl, is preparing for an extended visit to her sister who lives in the metropolis. This is where Sheinda and her grandparents are headed as well and arrangements are being made for her to join Chava in her sister's house.

PART III

SUMMER: 1943

SURVIVAL

CHAPTER EIGHT
THE METROPOLIS

Sheinda is standing in the kitchen facing the open window, her back to the room and to the young woman standing in front of the sink. She is watching the rain as it comes down in mighty torrents, its even trajectory disrupted time and again by gusts of driving wind. It's wild out there...but the spectacle has a calming effect on her emotions. She is glad to be inside — secure after the journey she and her grandparents have just concluded.

Their journey to the metropolis had been long and exhausting, but relatively safe. They traveled incognito, but in the open — in the same railroad cars with other legal passengers — their friends having obtained the necessary documents for them. After their arrival the grandparents were admitted to the communal old-age home and she came here — to this well-appointed city apartment — to live with the family Friedman.

The lady of the house is Chava's sister, but as unlike her as two sisters can possibly be. Like Chava, Mrs. Friedman is tall and slim, with more than a hint of the former's beauty and regal bearing. But she is very different in temperament, being somber rather than cheerful, and curt and imperial with the other members of the household — especially her servant.

The girl turns away from the window to face the young woman by the sink who has just finished washing the dishes.

"Can I help you dry?" she asks solicitously.

"No, Don't bother! I'm used to the work; the work is no problem, it's what I expected. It's the attitude that troubled me at first. But no longer. No, I'm really very grateful...glad to have a roof over my head and a bit of food when I'm hungry. After all, to them I'm really just a servant...a stranger who agreed to do their kitchen work. I know it is awkward for you — we are treated differently, you and I — but the main thing is we both have shelter."

"Yes, I know!" Sheinda whispers in comprehension but her mood remains grave. The situation is a real dilemma for her, for she finds herself slipping into the haughty manner the members of this household exhibit toward their servant. The thing that frightens her most is the ease with which she finds herself falling into that trap.

How shocked she had been the first time she entered this kitchen, an arrogant command in the manner of her hostess on her lips, to find that the maid doing the unpleasant work in the cold grubby kitchen, covered from head to toes by a coarse dirty apron, struggling with an enormous load of unwashed pots and pans was no other than her friend Rechi! Yes, Rechi, the girl from back home whom she befriended and who had been so decent to her.

Her first sensation upon seeing her friend was embarrassment. She was about to disappear, pretend that she didn't know her; it would have been easier than acknowledging her friend, now in the position of a servant, where she was a guest. She didn't heed her impulse to deny her friend, however. The impulse to deny was gone almost as soon as it appeared and she was able to greet her and return her affection and warmth. Instead of avoiding her, she sought her out and they would spend time together whenever Rechi's chores allowed her to do so. But Rechi insisted and she agreed that their friendship ought to remain a secret; their secret...something they alone shared. And so it was. She marveled at the ability of her friend to go about her work — work she wasn't used to, that was beneath her, really — with composure and sweetness offering comfort to others whenever she could. Sheinda, too, was able to partake in that comfort, but only much later did she come to comprehend and appreciate the true magnanimity of Rechi. Rechi may have become a servant, but her manner was that of a queen.

The old-age home her grandparents found a place in was part of a larger complex supported by the Jewish community. A few houses away was the main structure, the hospital, the major health facility in the city under Jewish auspices. Both facilities had been well equipped and efficiently run; institutions the community had taken great pride in establishing, though of late there were some difficulties in maintaining the standards.

The grandparents occupied a spacious, high-ceilinged room, on the first floor of this mansion-like structure. The walls were bright; they may have been freshly painted, with white, glossy woodwork. Although the furnishings were sparse, the room looked neat and well cared for.

A wide stone, perhaps marble stairway led up from the lobby on the lower level to the first, and higher floors. Ascending to the first floor, one landed in a long hall that stretched away to the right and to the left of the stairway. Both wings had several rooms facing, or diagonal from each other. Each was occupied by a couple, family, or single individual, several of them prominent refugees from abroad who were in the same situation as the grandparents. Most of them on this floor were people in their sixties and seventies, but all were in relatively good health, for the ill were cared for in the adjoining hospital.

There was the widow Berkowitz, the former wife of a rabbi, who had been living here for some years. She and her friend, Mrs. Bialer, the wife of Rabbi Bialer, lived across the hallway from the grandparents in adjoining rooms on the left side of the hallway. The Bialers lived in a large room they shared with a son, a youth of about twenty and a daughter, a petite, teenage girl with curly dark hair.

Other occupants in the home were Rabbi Morgenstern and his wife who lived — in adjoining rooms with their daughter Mrs. Blau and her two children — on the right side of the hall. Mr. Blau, the father of the two children, wasn't with them.... The Morgensterns and their family had also recently arrived from abroad.

Across the hall from them lived Miss Kränzler, a spinster in her eighties, one of the longest occupants of the home. Miss Kränzler, or Freulein Kränzler, as she liked to be addressed, was a graceful lady who carried herself with dignity. Her fine, snow-white hair was still all there: arranged in a plait, like a crown, around her head. She was thin, gaunt looking and tall, but with a straight back and her features revealed signs of former beauty. Unlike her neighbor Mrs. Nussbaum, a widow of long standing who was an extremely private, somewhat morose person, Freulein Kränzler was friendly and engaging: She liked to hold forth on themes involving her spinsterhood.

"I know," she once told Sheinda, "that I have missed many of the pleasures of family life. I haven't experienced the delights one gets from children of ones own. But then, I have also missed all of the sorrows; do you see what I mean? I missed the whole ball of wax: the good and the bad!"

The occupants were responsible for tidying their rooms on a daily basis, but thorough monthly cleaning was seen to by the staff. The living quarters had no separate kitchens. Some fruits and other snacks were allowed into the rooms, but major meals were prepared by the staff in the large kitchen and served in the communal dining room, both on the lower level. The food was good: appetizingly prepared, nourishing and fairly substantial. Sheinda loved it and since she spent a fair amount of her time with her grandparents, she was regularly invited to partake in the meals.

Several among the older women, Mrs. Berkowitz, Mrs. Bialer and Freulein Kränzler, occupied their spare time by knitting gloves — white gloves made of Angora yarn — which they sold to local merchants by the dozen. The girl was invited to join them whenever they met for this activity and she liked being present: not so much to learn their craft — although she managed to improve her skill considerably — as to listen in on their conversations which concerned current community affairs in general and some of the institutional gossip in particular.

She learned, among other things, of strenuous attempts being made by the Jewish leadership to make some deal with the enemy; to save people already in peril and to prevent deportation to the East of the Jews in this land. There were hopes of access to people in control, but no one seemed to know what the real prospects were.

She learned much about human relationships, as well, and began to form her own opinions and attitudes vis-a-vis the various occupants of the home. She became especially close with Mrs. Berkowitz, who took her under her wing, so to speak, and who made it her business to look after the girl's interests. She became close friends also with the Bialers and especially their daughter Lily, a vivacious girl fun to be with.

The manager who administered the home was Alice, a woman of about twenty eight, from the northeastern region recently annexed by the state. She had been living in the metropolis for several years, working her way up from relatively minor work to her present, responsible position. She was competent, self assured and attractive.

Recently two of Alice's sisters had joined her in the city. Alice managed to secure work for them both: the younger, Rosie, under her own supervision in the home. Rosie was a striking young girl of about seventeen, fairly tall and of athletic build, she was suntanned, her dark-golden skin contrasting nicely with her large, hazel eyes and light brown hair. Her mouth was wide and when she laughed, which was often, she revealed two lines of healthy white teeth. Rosie was also a good-hearted and genuinely kind person. She liked to work around people; performed her tasks diligently, with good cheer and soon became everyone's darling.

Young men began to appear on the scene, seeking to court and to date her. Alice, realizing that they were a fact of life, took the situation in stride, but sought to maintain control in this, as in all other affairs concerning the sisters in her care. She had a serious talk with Rosie, who agreed to date only young men of impeccable background and honorable intentions and to leave the screening process to Alice and the other adults in the home. Thus it happened that Rosie's affairs became everyone's business. Everyone took an interest, wanting to share in the excitement of her romantic activities.

It is late on a Wednesday afternoon. Dinner has long been finished; the dining room cleared of people and tidied up. The occupants, most of whom took a nap in the afternoon, would normally be seen emerging from their private rooms on the way to, or already engaged in, their various after dinner activities.

Not so today. Sheinda has just come down from her grandparents' room and sees that they are all assembled in the sewing room where Alice is supervising the seamstress in some special task. What, in Heaven's name, is going on? What is so important as to require the supervision of Alice, not to mention the presence of them all at this activity? What is the seamstress doing that holds such excitement for everyone? Why, the seamstress is indeed engaged in something extraordinary, the girl soon discovers. She is putting the last touches on a lovely new outfit for Rosie, because Rosie is going out tonight.... Yes, Rosie has a date; the long awaited event the success of which everyone has been agonizing over for weeks, is finally coming to pass....

Rosie steps out of the bathroom. She is freshly scrubbed with shining hair, sparkling eyes and a complexion turned pink and glossy. Now Alice steps up to her and situates her in front of a mirror where she applies make-up to her face and arranges her hair into an elaborate evening coif. A lovely pearl comb at the nape of her neck matches the strand of pearls she places around Rosie's neck. The seamstress is approaching with the dress from which she has just removed the last superfluous stitches and is handing it to Alice, who is to help Rosie into it.

This is the moment they have all been waiting for. No sooner has Rosie, with the vigilant help of Alice, managed to slip into and button the dress, than loud gasps of approval greet her from every corner; from all assembled. Rosie, after one last enchanted look at herself, steps away from the mirror. She makes her way to the middle of the room so as to afford a better view of herself to everyone then turns, and walks to and fro, in the manner of a model, ending with a curtsey and a final bow. The dress is white, setting off Rosie's beautiful tan, and is made of a sheer chiffon-like fabric with a wide, rose-colored band across the waist and a matching flower gracing the left side of the V-shaped neckline. Her hair, her pearls and her shoes complement the dress — taken together they transform her into a lovely apparition and she is amply applauded by all present.

The young girl looks at her with admiration mixed with a sense of longing. "I'm too young for this..." she thinks "but it isn't only my age, is it? I'm not unappealing, I know that, but I lack her charm...her physical beauty! I will never be sought after in the manner Rosie is, no! But, perhaps that will be a blessing to me, to have no admirers, I mean. I know I'll be forbidden to date. I will have to follow some different, special standard in this, as in all other things!"

These thoughts flash through her mind as she is joining the others in surrounding Rosie who is walking toward the vestibule where the young man, her date, is waiting. As she approaches, he rises, walks toward her, and offers her a small bouquet of violets. She takes the flowers, thanks him and gives them to Alice who places them among other freshly cut flowers on a special cart in the dining room. The young man is charming: he is tall, with classic features and wavy, light-brown hair. He must be in his early twenties, but looks quite a bit younger. Like Rosie he is formally dressed. He wears a well-fitting dark-gray suit, a sparkling white shirt and navy blue tie. He seems shy, inclining his head repeatedly as Rosie announces his name by way of introduction.

Alice, sensing the discomfort of both young people, comes to the rescue. She hands Rosie her wrap, entreating her not to be late. The young man follows her cue: he quickly opens the door, holds it until Rosie has slipped through it, then steps out after her and silently lets it fall behind them. Outside, he smiles at Rosie, who turns toward him a radiant face. He offers her his arm and guides her gently down the steps and out into the street.

Another lovely young girl who becomes Sheinda's role model in this large city is her friend Esti. Esti is here with her family: her elderly parents, with whom she lives in a small flat, around the corner from the old-age-home. Esti is their youngest, one of seven, but doesn't show the signs of a spoiled, youngest child. No, indeed. She is a very bright, self-possessed young person, somewhat chunky in physique, but very pretty with long auburn curls, a pert red little mouth and dark eyes. Esti is high-spirited, has much to say on every conceivable topic and takes on her young friend in the manner of a born teacher.

Esti's parents are very pious people, especially her mother, who is inspiring in her devotion. She makes it her business, more so than any other individual the girl has thus far encountered, to translate and explain the import of the various prayers she is reciting. Some of it makes a lasting impression. Sheinda has never forgotten the meaning of the short prayer (*V'-ani te-fi-lo-si l'cho a-do-shem*) preceding the *Amidah* of the *Shabbat Mincha* service: "I offer my prayer to you Hashem (an epithet for God, "the name"), at this time of special grace. O Lord, in your abundant kindness, answer me with your true help.

She often sees before her — as she recites the prayer — the image of that lady: a short, squat woman with a round face and uneven homely features that give her face a distorted look, but whose devotion and animation render her beautiful. That's what the girl remembers about her: her words, her reverence, her humble submission to the fate the Almighty has in store for her and her sense of duty to impart those feelings and what she knows to be the truth, to those around her.

The members of that family are very close. Occasionally, one or another of the married sons with families of their own, come to visit their parents and Sheinda is repeatedly astounded at the extraordinary homage these people accord their elders. She knows, of course, that their behavior is in line with the tradition — the way of life she grew up with — but they seem to her to come closer to the ideal than anyone she knows.

Esti takes her young friend for long walks around the neighborhood, mostly on Sabbath afternoons when there is little else to do. They say the required afternoon prayers and then they are free to roam. She becomes familiar with this part of the city: its streets, square, parks and playgrounds. This part of the city looks rural; it has much residential territory with gardens and parks and only scattered business establishments here and there. Most big business and industry is located in the twin city across the bridge. The two of them walk in the sunshine and sit in the shade. They watch little children at play and old people taking their afternoon walks, or sitting on park benches talking to each other. Often they run, chasing each other until they are out of breath, collapsing, finally, into some patch of grass where they can stretch out and catch their breath. Throughout it all Esti keeps the conversation going, chattering away and keeping her young friend amused: She tells her stories, recites poems, riddles and jokes. They sing, teaching each other the special songs associated with their various school experiences. Esti is a great friend to have around; she is cheerful, happy and her happiness is infectious; it brings much needed gladness to her friend who is less outgoing and is given to introspection and solitude.

CHAPTER NINE
THE HOSPITAL

It happens, at times, that Sheinda has no place to sleep. Her sojourn with the family Friedman was a temporary arrangement that ended recently. She now spends most of her time in and around the old-age-home. The inhabitants have adopted her; they provide her with concerned care and companionship, even food. But lodging is a problem, for she isn't officially eligible to live there. Nevertheless, the management knows that she often sleeps here (sharing the grandmother's bed) and makes it their business to notify the grandparents whenever a vacancy occurs. This is often the case in the nearby hospital, where patients are transitory, rather than in the old-age-home, where occupants have come to stay.

One day the grandparents are informed that a bed has been vacated in the hospital and she can sleep there tonight. So far, no patient has appeared to claim it, and even if someone does show up, it is hers for tonight. Good, she knows the procedure; she has been through it before. She packs her little overnight bag and walks over.

The room she is shown into is on the ground floor. It is a room with a single bed in it — a private room of sorts. Swell, she will be on her own; better than last time when she had to listen to the groans and witness the agony of people she couldn't help; people whose pain she was unable to alleviate.

The room has been freshly cleaned and smells of the carbolic substances used by hospitals. She dislikes the strong odor, the unfamiliar aspect of the solitary hospital room and the association of both with illness and death. She has the vague feeling that somewhere nearby — perhaps in the alley behind her window? No, no! It must be on the other side...yes, she remembers now... behind the room directly across the corridor from hers — is the morgue, the place where they take the people who die here.... Well, she mustn't think about that…she will do as she must; at least it isn't behind her window…as it was last time!

She looks around the room again, locates the W.C., the sink; then slowly moves toward her bag which stands on the floor near the bed. She opens it, removes her nightgown, slippers and toothbrush, places each within easy reach, then shoves the empty bag under the bed. Satisfied, she leaves the room and walks toward the nurses' station intent upon finding someone to talk to.

The nurse, writing behind the counter as she approaches, doesn't recognize her. Although most of the staff have seen her and are familiar with her status as recent refugee being given shelter here, there are part-time people who don't know her and she finds it necessary now and again to explain herself to them. She has to do that now, but finds the individual she talks to — a woman in her early thirties — very sympathetic to her problem and well informed about the ins and outs of hospital regulation.
She tells Sheinda that the best thing for her to do at the moment would be to have herself officially admitted as a patient.

"Don't you have some ailment — some chronic condition in need of treatment?" she asks. We have some very fine surgeons here; some are world famous, you know, people with patients all over Europe…. Should you wish to have your appendix removed, for instance, or some other operation you may need, you will find this the best place to do it in.

"Thank you," the girl responds, with misgiving. "I don't think I wish to have my appendix removed. No, my appendix is fine. I wouldn't want to disturb it. Is there anything else you may suggest for me to consider?"

"Well, let me see; I have mentioned other operations: we do have an excellent cardiac team, of course. They do surgery on the heart, you understand? But these would be very serious operations — undertaken only in cases of serious heart failure. We wouldn't want to subject you to one of those."

"Of course not" the girl agrees…"what else do they do here?"

"Gall and kidney stones, but those are also problematic operations."

Yes, they must be, she thinks, or Mama wouldn't have been so afraid to have it done. "Mama, where are you now? You should be here instead of me," she thinks; "they could take care of your problem here: free you of all that pain, all that suffering!"

"What about your tonsils?" the nurse continues, "Are they enlarged? Have you had problems with throat ailments?"

"Yes, I do! I mean I'm very often ill because of my tonsils... sometimes very ill. My tonsils get very swollen and white, I cannot swallow and I run a high fever."

"Good! No, I mean for our present purpose it is good that you have some malady that needs to be treated! I will see what I can do to arrange a bed for you."

The nurse was true to her word. She made an appointment with the surgeon who saw the girl that same afternoon. Her tonsils, he established, were not only large, but full of pus and should be immediately removed. They registered her as a patient and went through with the operation within a few days.

The first few hours after surgery were quite unpleasant: The wound was bleeding; the process of bringing up the discharge was painful. She could neither swallow nor talk and the taste in her mouth was not good, to put it mildly. But she faced it all bravely, glad that for the space of an entire week she had a legitimate place — a room of her own — without having to worry about a bed for the night.

She became something of a celebrity, as well. Not so ill as to occasion concern, but sufficiently so to merit attention, which she received aplenty — both from the hospital staff and her friends in and out of the nursing home.

On the day she was being discharged, she decided to make the rounds, stopping by the various rooms to take leave of the patients she had met. One of her acquaintances was absent from her room and since she had to wait Sheinda decided to visit and befriend some of the people in the adjoining rooms.

She is walking along the corridor and stops in front of a closed door. She waits a moment, listening to hear some movement, but there is no sound coming from within. She knocks lightly and waits, expecting to be invited in, but there is no response. She decides that the room is probably unoccupied and opens the door ever so slightly, expecting her suspicion to be confirmed. But no, the bed isn't empty, as she had anticipated. There is someone in it. She takes a few steps toward the bed and looks. What she sees has a most shocking effect, freezing her to the spot she stands on.

It is a small rectangular room with a large window facing the door. Behind the window is the alley with the morgue. By the wall, to the right side of the window is the white hospital bed. Lying on her side, covered by a light blanket with her face turned toward the window, is a youngish woman. Her hair is a dull brown tangled wet mass. Her brow is covered with sweat. Her face is sunken and a striking yellow in color.... Her mouth is open and from it there trickles — has evidently just stopped trickling — a thin stream of red blood! The figure on the bed is motionless. It is obvious that she is dead...she must have just died...!

The girl runs from the room, propelled by her fright and revulsion at the scene she has just witnessed. The staff calms and consoles her, explaining that the patient in question suffered from terminal cancer of the throat. Everything that could be done was done for her, they argue, but the shock was too great — she simply wasn't prepared to witness; to suddenly be brought face to face with this type of occurrence.

She goes back to the home, sleeping in a different place every night: more often than not in the hospital. She has grown used to it; takes the routine in her stride, happy that whatever her personal discomfort she is not alone at least, or in a concentration camp somewhere — the fate of her friends and relations....

Here life has assumed a semblance of normalcy. The local Jews, though subject to restrictive legislation and reduced circumstances, still live at home. The government, officially allied with the enemy, is dragging its feet on implementation of the harshest laws against its Jews. While it is clear that they harbor no love for them, their hate for those with whom they collaborate is such that they risk sabotaging anti-Jewish decrees even if that ends up benefiting the Jews.

One day the grandparents hear about Uncle Simon. Visitors from home and other acquaintances keep coming to visit — seeking advice and solace from the grandfather. One such visitor brings the news — both disturbing and hopeful. Uncle Simon has been sighted.... He is believed to have made the rounds: to have been shipped from one work camp to another, finally landing in Buchenwald where he is believed to be at present.... Somehow, word has it, he managed to get the message out — to let the world know...hoping that some contact can be established. If only they could notify the family, he is supposed to have pleaded.

Well, he succeeded! The family was notified, they are relieved to have some news that he lives and struggles against his fate! They are also glad to know where he is, crucial information if they are going to attempt to do something about it!

To do something...yes, they want to, very much. But how helpless they are! The grandfather informs every one of his supporters entreating them to do all they can. They assist him in undertaking a money-raising campaign. That is a first step and, as it turns out, the easiest. Money abounds...but it is of little help in turning around the inevitability of their fate. Since it is generally understood that you cannot approach anyone without the necessary funds, it is easily given.

Hence the grandfather and his collaborators manage to assemble a large fund. As soon as they have the funds in hand they establish contacts with certain highly placed officials known to be accessible who promise to intervene. Yes, the money is everywhere accepted and assurances readily given. And why not? It doesn't cost them a thing to promise. Yes, they will see to it. They are dispatching a courier as soon as possible; he will carry instructions for Uncle Simon's release. Not to worry, he will leave as soon as feasible...as soon as all details are worked out.

"All you need to do now is sit back and wait," one such official tells them. Too glib, too easy to be credible. Soon the money is gone and they are left with nothing but a bit of hope to which they cling desperately, against all odds, but which turns to nothing!

"We did all we could," the officials claim when challenged about the outcome. (Perhaps they did, who knows?)

"It's the people over there...in the camp. They are at fault; they won't let him go!"

Uncle Simon is not released, nor even heard from. He is left fighting on, with his last reserves of energy, struggling desperately to survive, while they — all those engaged on his behalf— wait and do nothing. There isn't a thing they can do: not for him; not for the others. It isn't only their torturers — those who decreed the laws, rounded up the victims, shipped them out and keep them there — who fail to respond; the rest of the world is also indifferent! Not a finger is being lifted anywhere to help, even though the truth has been known for some time, and enormous efforts are being made by groups of Jewish leaders to obtain cooperation of those who could help, if only they would!

PART IV

WINTER: 1944

RETURN

CHAPTER TEN
FLIGHT

She is up very early this morning, animated once again by the urgency of the moment. Events have caught up with them here too. The enemy is here! Their troops have moved in...have been in town since the night before last and, as everywhere else, have brought their terror with them. People are scrambling now to get away...those who can...who have somewhere to go!

For them, her grandparents and herself, the wisest thing is to return...to cross the border once again. In order to succeed, they must move fast...as soon as possible. This time they will not be going together! There is an opportunity for Sheinda to join a group that is leaving this very afternoon. They have agreed to take on one more person and she is ready! Her small backpack stands by the door prepared. She is alone in the room — having taken leave of the grandparents, for whom passage is being arranged for tomorrow — waiting for her contact to arrive.

"Take care of yourself; remember that in order to serve the Almighty we must survive! This is our First Commandment these days!" the grandfather counseled. "Dead people cannot serve the Lord. So, do what you must in order to stay alive! We hope to see you soon..."

The grandmother cried, but managed to bring her emotion under control so as not to upset the girl, and pressed a bar of chocolate and a small apple into her hands. They left the room, deeming it wisest to be discreet. She looks around the room as she waited. She has grown used to it, this room.... Not home, exactly, but part of the complex they had found shelter in and a sense of security no matter how fleeting. The people here, her friends who were so good to her, what will become of them...where will they go...?

The worst part of it all is the hurry: there is no time to take leave of any of them. Moreover, it isn't advisable to do so; suddenly it is every individual for himself again.

She doesn't have long to wait. There is a knock on the door and in walks her escort, the individual who is to take her to the assigned place. He is a young man of about twenty-eight, short in stature but with a slender elegance unobscured by the urgency of the moment.

"Hello," he says as he approaches. "Good, you're ready, no need to waste time — I'm Dov, by the way. I'm the one who organized the trip." He picks up her pack, helps her place it on her back and smiles, revealing a set of strong white teeth. She feels calm in his presence.

"Are you coming with us?" She asks.

"No, not on this run, not yet, I'm needed here, but my sister is going; I'm sending her home. There are other young people you will like and there will be the guide, of course!" She asks no further questions, intent on preventing further delay. She takes one last look around the room and they start on their way, silently closing the door behind them.

She is at the railroad station, having been brought here by Dov who introduced her to the others with whom she is to make the trip, gave them all last minute instructions and left. The group is composed of two middle-aged couples and several singles — including Dov's sister Rena and a young man by the name of Eli, the son of a well-known rabbi.

She looks at their guide who stands on the platform a few paces removed from the rest of the group — in an obvious attempt to distance himself from them; from any apparent association with them. He is a tall, thin young man with a shock of wavy blond hair. His face is somber and inscrutable; his manner inhibits discourse or any sort of inquiry they might have.

The members of the group have also scattered, standing in two's or individually along the length of the platform. Having arrived early, they have the platform to themselves for a while, but are soon joined by workers returning from their jobs in the city to the outlying communities of the metropolitan region. Many of these are blue-collar workers, carrying their heavy gear, who greet each other and exchange shoptalk. They appear surprised at the numerous strangers waiting for the train, and every now and then Sheinda notices one or another of them directing a suspicious glance in their direction.

"Not so good! We're too conspicuous!" she muses, but knows that there is nothing to be done; they will have to stick it out! The train will soon arrive, the group will scatter within its various compartments; these workers, settling in and attending to their own concerns will soon forget about them. The main thing is to sit apart from each other, remain silent and inconspicuous.

They all carry documents stating that they are Polish citizens (of non-Jewish descent) looking for work in rural parts of the state. The Polish Consul here, an individual disposed to help save the lives of Jews, cooperated in providing these documents. But they all know that these provide merely an illusion of security — good as long as they aren't needed.

Sheinda gets on the train, walks through several compartments and finally takes an isolated seat in a corner. She looks around and is glad to find only one other member of the group — the rabbi's son — occupying a seat in the opposite end of her compartment. Good! The two of them, at least, are doing their part; hopefully the others too have scattered and intermingled with other passengers. She sighs, closes her eyes and takes a deep breath. She is tired, but sleeping is out of the question: she will have to maintain her vigilance.

The train has been filling up; her compartment is packed by now. The passengers are mostly men, but there are a few women and even some children. Everyone is in a seat by now; the last few passengers who entered late having just placed their belongings above, or on the floor near their seats. The commotion and din occasioned by these activities are subsiding now as all attempt to find some comfort in the cramped spaces at their disposition.

On the seat across from Sheinda sits a young woman, a farmer's wife, judging by her attire, with an infant in her lap. The child woke up crying and the mother, attempting to soothe it, sticks a finger in its mouth and rocks it back and forth, but the foil doesn't seem to work: the infant makes several visible attempts to get its nourishment from the object in its mouth — without the desired result. It then lets out an anguished wail of disappointment, which is gaining in intensity. The mother, realizing it cannot be

111

avoided, bares her breast and offers it to the hungry infant. The baby, having at last found what it wants, commences to suckle in bliss.

The girl takes in the scene, her attention momentarily arrested by the mother and child and the absorption of each in this act of life-giving nurture. She cherishes the vision; it strengthens her illusion — begun upon her arrival at the train station and re-enforced by the bustle of activity on this train — that she is engaged in an ordinary excursion; on some trip temporarily away from home, where she is bound soon to return. She is determined to fully enjoy this semblance of normal life, as though she were truly part of it.

She leans back in her seat, looks out the window and observes the quaint panorama, the frames of landscape unfolding in rapid succession as the train speeds by. She sees sleepy villages, their huts indistinguishable from one another, huddled together, with a church steeple here and there protruding from the mass. Other structures fly by: sheds, barns, grain-storage buildings, bales of hay in the fields and cattle, some still at pasture, others, attended by shepherds, winding their way slowly to their village barns.

It is late afternoon of a balmy, winter day. Soon the sun will be setting, but now it is still some distance from the horizon, a golden ball in a sky full of orange yellow and purple, lending an enchanted glow to the vistas below. The girl sits mesmerized, her head turned toward the window, with barely a trace of awareness of her surroundings apparent. But these are only appearances. In reality her antennae are deeply sunk; so deep that she immediately becomes aware of the slightest threat, as if by instinct.

Presently something causes her to turn her head away from the window and she directs her gaze to the other end of the compartment where Eli, the rabbi's son is sitting. She can see that he is looking in her direction and although he is completely still, as if frozen in his seat, she can sense an agitation; a distinct anxiety pervading his being. She silently rises from her seat and makes her way toward him, as if on the way to the washroom. As she passes his seat she looks at him and having caught his gaze, motions imperceptibly toward the direction she is following. The young man nods. He is standing in the clearing in front of the washroom when she emerges.

"What is bothering you? I couldn't help noticing you have something on your mind." Her lips are barely moving, but her whisper is sufficiently distinct for him to respond:

"Yes, I worry over what's to happen to me once we are across the border. You see, I don't speak that language. I need someone to assist me, or I won't survive. Would you mind sticking with me for a while over there — long enough for me to find my way — I don't want to get caught before I even make it into the city...."

"Okay, I don't mind," she whispers. "I shall try to assist you for a while, until we must each go our separate ways. Do you remember the instructions we need in the meantime?"

"Yes! We are to follow the guide in getting off the train before it enters the station of...this village. I'm anxious about that. I've never gotten off a moving train before...."

"I know! I'm also worried; the best thing is not to think about it. You'll be fine."

She smiles and returns to her place.

Back in her seat, she tries to relax. All around her is quiet: Most of the passengers are dozing. The infant in its mother's lap is soundly asleep. She looks out the window again: the landscape hasn't changed; the villages, gardens and fields succeeding one an-other may be different ones, but they look much like those that preceded them. She closes her eyes.

The room is dark, the lights have been out for a while; they're all in their beds, but no one is sleeping.

"How about 'go to buy,' " it's her brother Chaim's voice. "We haven't played that one for a while."

Chaim is the oldest of the boys, only a year younger than she. He is easily the handsomest of them all. Chaim has her father's roundish face, shape of mouth and smile. But whereas her father has a dark, curly head and beard, Chaim's hair is a lustrous golden blond. His hair is all shaved off, of course, but his payes [side locks], arranged in two long dangling curls framing his face, show that his hair tends toward blond waves. Chaim has a rosy complexion, a chiseled, short nose and cherry red lips, but his best feature are easily his enormous blue eyes. Those are deep blue, the color of the sky on a clear, cloudless day. They are framed by heavy lids, ringed with long, golden lashes. He is the tallest of the children, but even so somewhat short for his thirteen years. But no matter: Chaim is outgoing, un-inhibited, given to action, not contemplation and they've all come to rely on him, even the parents, when anything special needs to be attended to. He is especially fond of, and often successful, in dealing with the local officials and is glad to render his service to friends and neighbors as well as his family. Where did he learn that skill? No one knows, or cares. The main thing is he is there, eager to do what's needed.

"Sheinda, you begin. Chaim after you, then me." The voice is that of Sheinda's brother Schmiltchu [Samuel], the gifted introvert. He is also blond and blue-eyed, his features resembling those of their mother, but lacking the radiant beauty of his older brother. He is a quiet, withdrawn boy who takes his studies seriously and is very devout. His sister can tell from the way he prays: with his eyes closed, a gartel [braided silken belt] around his waist; his custom-made kashket [round, black pillbox of a shiny, silken material] firmly on his head, he sways back and forth with ardor — not allowing anything to distract him until he is done. And he takes his time. Nothing is more important to him. For this and for his excellence in "learning" he gets much praise from all around him.

"A true yerei shamayim" [God-fearing person], Mama intones repeatedly and looks in his direction with pride. Daddy agrees and his heart swells. Schmieltchu is modest, unassuming, but he knows that his parents and his teachers expect much of him.

Schmieltchu has another asset: an unusually beautiful voice, a soprano, and he has mastered the chants and songs connected with prayer. Of late, friends and neighbors have been dropping in during the Sabbath meal, as soon as they hear him sing; for his clear, bell-like voice carries far and its beauty, everyone claims, is extraordinary — something not to be missed!

Sheinda, too, loves to hear him sing. His voice speaks to her of things he doesn't otherwise express: of passion and love within him and of beauty, compassion and hope.... For the last year or so her two brothers have been away from home. They are students at a yeshiva (center of learning) in a nearby city and are now home on one of their semester breaks. Schmieltchu has done exceedingly well, attending to his studies and earning praise from everyone. Chaim, less studious, has been in charge of their affairs. He sees to it that their lodging is comfortable, their room neat, their clothes properly folded and in their place. An innate collector, he throws nothing away, preserving every carton, wrapper and piece of string, in the claim that it may all come in handy one day. He maintains rapport with the school community, both fellow students and teachers alike, by attending to some of their needs as well. It is he who makes certain that they have invitations for the Sabbath meals at one or another of the prominent households in the community. Chaim takes care of all that and Schmieltchu "sits and learns."

"I'm also playing!" The voice is that of her sister Tzipora.

"No, you can't, not tonight. It's late and you take too long." Chaim retorts. Tziporah is insulted and begins to cry.

"Oh, come on, let her play! You're wasting time." Sheinda admonishes and reaches out to stroke her sister's shoulder.

"Okay," she calls out, "Go buy me a, let me see now, how about a barrel of wine, from — she gives no other clue as to where and from whom this is to be obtained. Since there are several shops in town, each with a number of people from whom wine can be purchased, they each take their turn guessing in response to further clues until they are stopped: either by an incorrect response or by providing the answer. They each get their turn posing the initial question and the game goes on until each drops out by falling asleep.

Tzipora had participated and she had done very well, eager to show her competence. Good girl, her sister muses. She glances at the sleeping child sprawled next to her and listens to her even breathing. Tzipora is sleeping on her right side, turned to the wall, her long blond hair covering her left shoulder. Her sister moves unconsciously toward the outer edge of the bed, turns to repose on her left side and shifts her eyes toward the crib, where her little brother Djudju [David] is sleeping.

Djudju, their youngest one. — Soon he too will be able to take part in their games. How time flies. He is five years old now and easily the brightest of them all, with a sense of humor rare in a child. No wonder he is the little darling; not only the family's but everyone else's. He is tiny: short and thin but he dashes about with a wonderful agility. He has an olive complexion, light brown hair and his dark eyes sparkle with animation and mischief.

She recalls the event of his birth. She can see everything so clearly. He was born in Mama's bed in the large bedroom. The midwife, Mrs. Blau, keeps coming in and out of the household. She is in charge of all that must be seen to before the event. She has Mama's bed stripped, scrubbed and dressed in white linen; an enormous red rubber mat spread on top of the sheet. On the table, now cleared of all other things, stand several trays with everything that will be needed during and after the birth: one of these holds cleanly washed instruments of some sort, which Mrs. Blau hopes will not be needed. The others are stacked with white linen towels, cotton napkins, diapers and rolls of cotton. There are basins with pitchers in them, a tin tub, fresh linen for the bed and several clean shirts and a bed jacket for Mama.

On one of the night tables, the one closer to Daddy's bed, the girl can see the new swaddling cloth. It is gleaming white, embroidered, with ruffles around the part that will go around the infant's head and shoulders. Along the lengths of its front edges (about three inches from the edge), there are long satin ribbons (three on each side) about three inches wide that will be tied into bows, after all edges have been tucked in snugly to hold the baby in place. Arranged in a circle around the swaddling cloth are little white shirts, jackets, a bonnet and socks. Some of these are old, but all have been carefully washed.

The preparations are now complete and the household lies in waiting. Maňa and the other help tiptoe around the house, so as not to disturb Mama and the midwife, at whose beck and call they now stand. The children have fallen into line, keeping out of the way; appearing only when called for, but excited with anticipation. They know that whatever is to come will happen soon. Their father has been home most of the day — having returned early — and is assisting with their care, a task he is used to. He goes in to speak with Mama, and comes out smiling, calming them. Mrs. Blau walks around the house surveying the situation: yes, everything seems in order. There are cauldrons of boiling hot water waiting on the stove; the utensils and implements she needs are all here: the linens, the extra cloths, fresh bedding, the apparel for mother and child, all have been prepared. Good! She is pleased. The preliminaries are now out of the way; this is the moment she has been waiting for — to do what she is here for; the work at which she is truly at her best.

She enters the room in which her client struggles in agony and stops, listening to her moan softly after a sudden bout with sharp pain. She slowly approaches the bed inquiring:

"How do you feel? Are we making any progress?"

"Yes, I think we are almost there. The pain is steady now, I think you ought to take a look."

The midwife looks and is startled by what she sees, for she rushes into action at once, summoning her assistants — to whom she had previously assigned specific tasks — as the very first step. She repeats her instructions, after which they all scurry into different directions to bring her what she needs. She herself rolls up her sleeves, places Mama into the position she needs to be in, and proceeds to put her at ease in order to lessen the pain and ease the final stages of the process. They are all in the front hall, awaiting the news. They don't have long to wait. The door opens suddenly exposing Mrs. Blau who announces with glee:

"A beautiful little boy." Mazel tov.

She opens her eyes to something of a commotion around her. The train is standing still, one of its routine stops, presumably. Some passengers have gotten off, others are getting on. She gets off her seat, stretches her rigid limbs, then decides to walk for a bit. She walks to the end of her compartment, then through the next and on, intending to survey the length of the train. She comes to a halt in the middle of one of them and looks around.

In the corner by the next door stands the young fellow, their guide: he is facing the window, seemingly intent upon the scene, but he has a far-away, distracted look, as though he were looking beyond the things in his view. He is whistling softly, and she recognizes the tune: it's the latest hit, imported by the occupying army and taken up with zeal by the local population, who even translated the words into their own language. The lyrics are an ode to true love — the only thing that allegedly survives all else.

She turns around to return to her seat, but stops suddenly, her attention taken by the three official-looking men in uniforms, probably the local gendarmerie, who have just entered. The three huddle with each other for a few moments, as if to divide a task among themselves, then scatter, each in a different direction.

The passengers who have gotten off at this stop are still on the platform, slowly making their way toward the village. The remaining passengers are either reposing in their seats, or are preparing to leave at the next station. The whistle has just sounded, the doors are in the process of closing and the train will soon be in motion again; she turns instinctively to look at the guide who, she realizes, has moved away from his corner by the window and is making for the door. Her gaze follows him as he stops, deftly pries open the door, jumps off the slowly moving train and disappears from view.

For a moment she stands there horrified! So their guide is gone ...and the police, probably looking for them, are on board. What to do? The best thing, she knows, would have been to get off when he did, but it's too late for that. The doors are now sealed and the train is moving at full speed.... She takes a few moments to reflect, then begins moving slowly and unobtrusively to her place on the train. As soon as she arrives, she lowers herself quietly into her seat in the corner, pulls a small, tattered blanket from her knapsack and brings it over her shoulders, partially covering her head and face. She pretends to be asleep. The woman and her infant are still sitting across from her. To onlookers, she may appear as part of their family. She waits.

Her compartment remains quiet, the passengers largely unaware of the drama soon to unfold. After about half an hour, the door to her compartment opens suddenly: one of the gendarmes who boarded the train at the last stop makes his appearance. He is a tall man clad in the uniform, with matching hat, of the rural police. He makes his way slowly, sweeping the passengers with his gaze, but keeps on moving. He doesn't stop — apparently satisfied that no unusual, suspicious characters are present here. Her heart is pounding wildly as he moves by her seat...letting his glance linger at her for a brief moment, then wander away indifferently, as he makes his way into the next car.

Her fellow travelers are less fortunate. They are all-too conspicuous: their dress, their manner, the fear plainly written on their faces, give them away. They might have slipped by had there been no inquiry. But this raid seems to have been a search for them, for their party. Apparently someone suspected them, and alerted the authorities. They are caught, rounded up, and taken off the train at the very next stop.

She looks out the window and sees the entire group, including Dov's sister — Dov, who arranged this escape — as they are marched off the station, surrounded by gendarmes. She is filled with horror. All their struggles, all their hopes now gone and she, should she succeed in reaching her destination, will have to bear the terrible tidings; will have to confront Dov's parents and tell them of the fate that befell their child. And they will have to place her...find a place in town for her safety...what a tragic irony! She turns toward the window and closes her eyes, so as to hide the tears welling up in her eyes. She must pretend to be as indifferent to the tragedy she has witnessed as the rest of the passengers who, judging by their comments, take it in their stride. To them, perhaps because they are expected now to take indecencies against Jews in their stride, the event is merely an inconvenience — an unexpected interruption of their journey. None seem surprised; some express annoyance at the delay, others remain silent, minding their business. There are no expressions of pity, or of sorrow: if there are any on this train who have such sentiments, they have succeeded in hiding it.

She looks up, suddenly, recalling that she didn't see the young man, Eli, among the group taken off the train. Where is he? Is it possible that he, too, has escaped detection? She doesn't know and doesn't want to find out. All she knows is that she must take her few things together, have her little pack in readiness and leave this train as soon as she can safely manage. The young man in question will have to fend for himself, just as she must.

Her problem now is that she doesn't know the name of the designated station; she doesn't know where it was they were supposed to leave the train, nor the name of the party in the village who was to assist them. No, she is all alone now, her destiny once again in her own hands!

She sits quietly, struggling with her emotions in an effort to get them under control. As soon as she feels safe to do so, she gets up and moves to a vacant seat right next to the door, preparing those around her that she is soon to depart. She waits for another stop to come and go, then steels herself for what she must do. She stands in the narrow space between compartments and waits for the train to slow down. It would be good to do as their guide had done — pry open the door before the train pulls into the station, but this is impossible; she doesn't have the physical strength. She decides to wait for the train to stop, which will be very soon now, to be the first off the train, leave the station platform immediately; find some side exit and head for the fields.

The train has come to a halt and the doors have opened. She adjusts the pack on her back and casts one last look into the train before making her exit. Among the passengers behind her about to descend from the train is the young man, the rabbi's son. He is looking at her, watching her movements, and she realizes that he intends to, will almost certainly follow her. What to do? His presence complicates matters; it renders her prospect of slipping away undetected a bit more difficult. She pretends not to see him and acts as if she were alone, hoping to put some distance between them so as to minimize danger to them both. She steps off the train and hurries away.

They have been walking for a long time. The narrow, crooked path they are on leads through a meadow with nothing to see on either side. She peers into the distance ahead of them, hoping to discern some sign of habitation, but there is nothing. All she can see in the twilight are brown and yellow patches of frozen ground with a bare, denuded tree or hedge at intervals along the way. The sun is now gone, but night has not yet arrived: a strange, eerie glow lingers, lighting their way.

"I think we should rest for a bit. Do you think it is safe now?" It's the young man speaking. For about half the distance since the station they have been walking together; he having caught up with her. She didn't mind now, as long as they were on their way...she did promise to assist him and it's better than being totally alone in the night.

"I don't know if it's safe, but we aren't safe walking either, are we? We might as well take a few minutes to rest, but where? Do you see anywhere we might sit down?"

"How about that large tree over there?"

She agrees. They sit on the tattered blanket she pulled from her bag, folded in half, so as to form a barrier between them and the frozen ground they're sitting on, and rest. After a short while Sheinda asks:

"Have you got any money?"

"Some, why do you ask?"

"We want to be prepared! Should we be lucky, I mean should we find someone to assist us, we will have to pay. I will have to be the one to talk to them, since you're mute — remember? The less we need to talk to each other, the better."

The young man pulls out his wallet, removes the bills it holds and counts them. There are ten altogether. He removes five and hands them to the girl:

"I'm afraid this is all I can spare — I must leave something-"

"Of course," she counters, taking the bills from him. She opens her bag and removes a small leather pouch holding her own money. She removes a few bills, folds them and with her back to her companion carefully places them into the upper part of her undergarment. She puts the rest of her money together with his bills back into the pouch and returns it to its place in her pack.

They sit a while longer. She looks around her, scanning the surroundings. She peers into the distance in every direction, but can see nothing. They are evidently still some miles from any habitation and it is getting dark. They will have to get on with it.

"Let's go," she says as she rises to her feet. The young man follows suit. They help each other with their bundles and reluctantly resume their trek.

It is now pitch dark. They are in an orchard leading to what appears to be a farmhouse. It is the first dwelling they've come to. She has no way of knowing what she will find, but they must try.

They make their way to the door of the dwelling; she steps forward and knocks several times at the door, whispering to her companion as she does so:

"Remember, you're mute — no talking!"

"Very well," says the young man and they wait.

Presently the door is yanked open and a young fellow clad in overalls on top of a tattered flannel shirt confronts them.

"Yes?" he inquires, "staring at them curiously, his unuttered questions hanging in the air between them. It is clear he wishes to know who they are and what business they have with him at this time of the night? Sheinda steps forward:

"We're refugees. We're coming from the distant metropolis trying to get back home — across the border, you know?"

"You're lucky it's me — I mean us, our family. We come

from the same region you do — but, I'm sorry to tell you, there is still the border to cross if you're going there."

"Thank you, at least you can understand me!" she counters. Could you, or someone in your family possibly help us — take us across, I mean? We will make it worth your while...will give you all we have!"

"Tell you what — why don't you follow me," he recommends and leads the way to an adjoining structure; a little shed housing various farm implements.

"I'll inform my family — tell them of your need — and we will see what can be done. They will have to be prepared," he says and winks conspiratorially..."especially my mother. She won't like the idea of my trudging across borders in the night — but I know what the best way is...I've done it before! Why don't you two just sit here awhile and relax! Who is the young fellow?"

"He is my brother; he's mute, but he's smart. He won't be a problem."

"Well — sit down why don't you? I'll get you two something to eat, but first let me see what I can do to swing my folks." He leaves them sitting on their packs in a corner of the toolshed.

"Could have been worse!" It's Sheinda whispering. "I think the young fellow wants to do it —"

"Yes—" begins her companion but stops abruptly, as she puts her finger to her lips indicating silence! Of course, he mustn't talk...no one must hear him.

They sit for a long time; interminable, it seems, before the fellow returns. When he finally does, he brings some bread, milk and cheese with him. They're starved — having eaten hardly anything for most of that day. They fall to it ravenously, the lad watching them devour the food. After they're done, he inquires:

"How much have you got? You will have to pay in advance. Once you do, I'll find you a place to sleep for awhile before we start. We'll have to leave soon after midnight — there's no time to lose. I'll take you across! But once you're there you'll be on your own. I'll have to return then — I can only go until a certain point. Are we agreed?"

"Fine with us!" the girl offers and proceeds to locate her money pouch. When she does, she empties it of its contents and hands the money to the lad saying:

"This is all there is. We have no more! Will this be enough?" He counts the bills she handed him and frowns:

"I got twice as much last time — it's hardly worth the bother; I don't know..." he mutters reflecting, his brow furrowed in disappointment. Could you send us the rest?"

"I don't know. Probably not — I might as well be frank.. this is all there is!"

"Well okay," he says at last, after what seems like an eternity — but they do seem to have a deal!

After they've rested, it is time to get under way. Their young collaborator comes to fetch them and takes them back to the main building. They enter a large, poorly lit room, but light enough to discern the whitewashed walls and the mud floor. Around a wooden table sit the other members of this family: the farmer and his wife and a couple of middle aged males — these are either relatives, or farm hands. The children of the household aren't present; they're obviously asleep.

The exchange that ensues concerns the business at hand. The girl has a chance to repeat her story: they're siblings from abroad returning home. Their parents are anxious — what with the foreign troops having taken over the capital city recently...All they want is for someone to take them across...show them the way; they'll manage the rest.

The farmer and his wife listen without interrupting her. They seem eager to hear the story. It is unclear whether they believe her, but seem pleased to hear an explanation: some plausible argument to cover their action, as it were.

"Good," says the farmer after a considerable lapse of time.

"You've eaten, haven't you? And you've rested a bit. You're ready to go, aren't you?"

Sheinda shakes her head in affirmation, after which the farmer's wife asks a few questions concerning her hometown, her parents and family. The girl has no trouble answering these questions — she knows the town she hails from well and is able to provide authentic detail. The farmer's wife, hailing from an adjacent region (as does her husband), is nostalgic about the land of her origin and its people. She is glad to speak Sheinda's language — her own mother tongue — and if she harbors any doubts as to the girl's true identity, as she well might — she makes no overt reference to it.

Presently she rises from her seat, entreats her son to be careful and leads the way in escorting the two refugees out of the house. They say goodbye at the fence and the farmer and his wife return to the hut. The two young people, accompanied by the young boy, depart.

The two of them have been walking for a long long time. It is a dark, moonless night. The air is damp; a cold drizzle is coming down steadily, soaking their light clothes. They're walking along the muddy bank of a brook now, their soggy shoes getting stuck in the mud time and again. It is slow going. The girl is shivering with cold and apprehension. The young fellow who brought them has departed some time ago. He simply pointed in the direction of a little path ahead of them stretching into the distance — the path they've since been following and advised:

"This is as far as I can go — I must return now. You'll be across very soon, just follow this path: don't stray from it, or you'll be returning to us. You're lucky it's quiet tonight; no one about to bother you...good luck!" He turned around and was gone!
They stood there alone in the cold miserable night feeling abandoned, not knowing what's awaiting them at the end of this journey. But they had no real choice. The only thing they could do was walk on, and so they did!

The wet chill is penetrating to their very bones, but the miserable weather has its advantages: it is safer for them, Sheinda reflects. Yes, they are cold, wet and so tired, but to think about all that now is a luxury she knows they can't afford. They keep on walking. After a long while she stops, puts down her knapsack and casts her eyes about in search of some place to rest a bit, but there is nothing in sight — nothing that might shelter them from either the elements or from prying eyes. No, they must walk on; soon it will be dawn, at which time they must be safely in some hiding-place — some shelter where they might remain until it is dark again. They resume their trek.

CHAPTER ELEVEN
IN SHELTER

She is here at last. After what seemed an interminable amount of walking they arrived at a little town and made their way to the railroad station. She knew at once that the border is behind them — could read the signs in the language she was looking for. The official at the counter behind the glass partition informed them that there should be a train to the city of their destination within the hour.

"Looks like you walked some distance to get here, didn't you? You can use the washroom to tidy up a bit," he advised, pointing them in the direction of the waiting room. They took his counsel and returned refreshed — though their clothes (which had to be rinsed to remove the grime) clung to them in their wetness.

The man didn't seem to suspect anything out of the ordinary. Apparently people walked to this station from far away, in all sorts of weather. They each found a quiet spot on the benches lining the waiting room walls and slept until it was time to board the train.

On the train she decided to act naturally, as though she had nothing to fear. She entered into conversation with a businessman next to them; told him of her flight from the metropolis across the border and how happy she was to be going home (her non-Jewish identity assumed, but not mentioned by either of them); obtained the information she needed concerning their destination: the town they were going to, he said, was several hours away. Once again the two of them separated and each found a place to stretch out in, on the sparsely occupied train.

Once again, they were off the train as soon as they could manage and headed toward town before anyone could apprehend them. The city was unfamiliar to her — she had never been here before. However, she carried with her the address Dov had given her; to the house of his parents and it seemed no great task to find the street they lived on.

Dov's parents lived in the center of town, in the Jewish quarter turned into a ghetto, along with all those remaining Jews who had been granted exceptions to the deportation. This particular city had always been a center of Jewish learning with a large yeshiva established and led by the local rabbi, a well-known Judaic scholar who, together with his brilliant son-in-law, managed to attract serious students from many regions of central Europe. This center of learning had been granted recognition and its inhabitants (both teachers and students as well as a host of service people necessary to maintaining the community) were granted a measure of protection: they were left in residence and were not deported. This protection was still in force as the girl and her companion arrived in the city.

Dov, the individual who came to get her for this trip had notified his parents of the transport he had arranged and they eagerly awaited their reunion with their daughter. It now fell to the girl to give them the dreadful news that their daughter was caught and taken off the train.... How terrible...how she hated to do it! She, a total stranger to them is here, looking toward assistance from them while their own child, their precious daughter, was gone perhaps never to return.

It so happened that her worst fears were realized. The parents were totally unprepared for the news and turned away from her in cold anger — as though the tragedy that had befallen their child were somehow her fault. No, of course not, they couldn't have thought so, and it wasn't anger — it was merely distance and indifference; they couldn't bear to see her because every glimpse of her brought home to them the horrid reality: here she was, intact and within reach and their own daughter...gone!

Her companion, the rabbi's son, found a place at the yeshiva. Sheinda found shelter with a local family whose teen age children had been sent to the camps, but they had another, a very young child, only a few months old. The master of the household was pleasant enough: he was a short man with a protruding belly and a round, smiling face. He was gone most of the day — supervising his former clothing store now under Aryan control. His wife, possibly his second spouse, was an obese young woman in her early thirties. She stayed in the house most of the day, but didn't do much work. She had help with the household chores and spent much of her time in idle pursuit: reading romances, gossiping with neighbors, or just sitting with her feet propped up. Good for her circulation, she claimed. She agreed to take in the girl; she gave her room and board in exchange for looking after the baby.

The baby, a little girl, was pudgy, pink and cute as a button. Sheinda took to her immediately and grew very fond of her. She would wheel her about in her large pram and sing her heart out while putting the little one to sleep. The baby came to depend on the routine and, after a while, wouldn't go to sleep without it.

Sheinda loved to do it. She became a familiar sight wheeling the baby around in the yard and in adjoining streets and she did it with pride; with a sense of self-importance. She felt needed; she was of use to someone: someone sweet, innocent and helpless. She would have remained with this family for the duration of her stay in that locality, were it not for the fact that the lady of the house, the baby's mother, took a sudden dislike to her. She began criticizing her rather destructively (perhaps she grew jealous of the baby's dependence on her). Sheinda complained to the communal leadership and it was decided to remove her from their custody. She much regretted to lose the baby to whom she had grown quite attached and was sorry for the baby. She knew she would be missed, but had to think of her own needs.

She is staying at the house of the Gordons, a middle aged couple with no children at home. The man, a tall, gaunt figure always dressed in black, is a rabbi from some distant community who found temporary shelter in this city. Both he and his wife are kind to her, but the rabbi makes it his special business to attend to her personal needs. She is embarrassed by this; she isn't used to having her water for the morning ablution of hands brought to her by an elder, especially a rabbi. But he insists, considering it a special privilege, as he assures her, to be of service to a member of her family. (She is a descendant of a rabbinic dynasty with many devoted adherents known as Hasidim.)

His attitude humbles her and she in turn tries to be of help to them in their solitude. There are no children at home now and the Gordons don't mention any, but Sheinda knows that they have some; she had heard references to a son. Where he is and what became of him she doesn't know. Was he forced into labor somewhere...God knows where? Perhaps this is no coincidence, she reflects. Could it be that she is here to bring some cheer to them, to brighten their life and console them? She doesn't know, but takes on this task as her current mission and tries to reciprocate their kindness as best she can.

Much to her chagrin she doesn't find it easy to act as a daughter. She is unable somehow to view them in the role of her parents. She is kind, polite and helps out in the house with as much cheer as she can muster, but at the same time remains somewhat aloof.

One morning, arriving home from the synagogue, Rabbi Gordon informs her that her uncle, with whose family she had visited (in the border city, on her way to the metropolis) is here in this town. She is amazed...and pleased to hear about it, but afraid, too, of the news he brings with
him. No one mentioned anything about his family; he is apparently here alone.

She immediately goes to see him; they meet at the entrance to the enclosure in which the yeshiva is located. Uncle Chaim has been assigned a function at the school and has a room in one of the dorms. He doesn't take her up to his room; they stand in the doorway to the building and he inquires about her welfare, then says:

"It's been a long time since we saw each other; it seems like from another age, the memory of your stay with us (approximately two years have passed since her visit). You, of course, were already in the midst of it: past the terrible separations, but for us it had not yet begun. We were still all together, remember? Still able to harbor the illusion of normal life. That's all over now. I'm alone here, just like you are and to tell you the truth, my heart isn't in it - to try and save my own skin, I mean."

She looks at him and a wave of compassion touches her heart. Uncle Chaim, who resembles her father, but is blond, had always been the shorter of the two. But his energy and agility of movement, his intelligence and wit combined to give him stature. His great presence tended to obscure his actual height. But no
longer. He appears shrunken in his grief — it is clear that he no longer is the man he had been. He still rushes about in his quick

128

nimble manner, but his face bears a sickly pallor and his movements, if not altogether devoid of energy, seem without purpose. He misses his wife and children, who were his entire life, with unusual intensity.

He doesn't go into details about their fate; doesn't want to. She does manage to find out that long before he left, the Jews had all been taken from their homes and herded into ghettoes at first, then shipped to the East. The Great Aunt, her little boy, Leah, his own family and everyone else in town had to go: there were no exceptions. A handful of people managed to hide or escape and he is one of them, but he is very unhappy; he carries about a great deal of guilt.

He bids her to wait for him a while and makes his way up the stairway to his room. She waits, wondering what he is about. In a short while he is back, with a little box wrapped in paper and tied up with string.

"Here, I think you should have this, you're the only female left of the family. It isn't mine — it was given to me by the Great Aunt just before they were shipped away. It contains what's left of her family jewels."

Sheinda opens the little box containing two items: a large, oval shaped gold pin studded with a row of large diamonds in the center and two rows of smaller stones on each side. It is an antique pin with a heavy eighteen-karat gold lining and stones of the old cut: the girl remembers the pin well; she had often admired it. The other item is a small envelope holding a bunch of loose, unstrung pearls of the uncultured variety. These had been part of the Shtern Tichel (tiara made of pearls) the Aunt had worn as part of her Schleier, the Friday night headdress donned by a rebetzin for the ceremony of lighting the candles. The girl views the objects with emotion, then replaces everything and puts the little box into her purse. She will take it with her, and guard it well.

A few days later, a letter arrived from the grandparents, who were now in the capital city. They, too, had come back across the border safely and, as it happened in the nick of time. A few days after they left, dreadful events occurred there, events that are exceptional in their cruelty even for the Germans. Both the hospital and the old-age-home — those two wonderful Jewish institutions where she and her kin had found shelter and dignity had been "liquidated" along with all other Jewish habitations. The occupants, it was rumored — whether young, old, healthy or ill, had been murdered: some burned alive in the fires set for that purpose, some shot in their beds, the rest driven away and drowned in the Danube.

All those beautiful people, her friends; whose generosity nourished her so and gave her such comfort. How eager they had been to help, never realizing what horrible fate awaited them. Sheinda couldn't get them out of her mind and saw their beautiful faces: Rosie, dressed as she had been for her date; the young man approaching her with the bouquet of flowers; Estie and her mother reciting the special Sabbath evening chant; the old men and ladies of the old age home with whom she had been so intimately connected. And the children...the countless young children of the community….all killed?

The Grandparents are pleading with her to join them in the ghetto of the capital city on this side of the border, where they are now living. She has been with the Gordons for a few weeks now and is beginning to feel at home. Her uncle is here, too, and they manage to see each other occasionally. This is the place she would have chosen to remain, were it not for the grandparents, who obviously need her. She is anxious to see them as well and she begins at once to make plans to leave.

She has only a few things to pack. Her old bag is ever ready and she places her few belongings in it with care. The taking leave, especially from her uncle, is accompanied by many tears. She knows the reality by now — most of these partings are forever... so she lingers over the frail image of her uncle, reluctant to go, bidding him to take care, but sensing that he is oblivious; she fears for him because he is so resigned. They embrace and he holds her to him, then smiles as they part, wishing to cheer her. She turns abruptly and leaves, never to see him again.

CHAPTER TWELVE
REUNION

She arrived in the large city late at night and, as prearranged, was met at the railroad station by a middle-aged man holding up a blank, white sheet of paper. This was to be her sign: a man holding up a white page. She found him soon after alighting from the train and they sped toward their destination.

They soon arrived before a large structure: a compound of old houses standing close together on one of the streets within the Jewish quarter of this old city, the city that now served as the state capital. They stopped at the portal to one of the houses in the street, a large oval-shaped doorway. This door turned out to be a gate that led them into a narrow passage surrounded by apartments on each side. They walked ahead a few meters and found themselves in a large square courtyard with dwellings huddled close together on the three sides of the square before them. Her companion headed for the long wrought iron terrace stretching horizontally in front of them that bound the many dwellings in this row together. They approached the terrace from the right and mounted the stairs leading unto it, then continued on ahead stopping in front of the door at about the middle of the row.

"This is it! Here is where your grandparents live." said the man. "Why don't you just knock on the door; I live just a few apartments away and must leave you now. Good luck," he added, then discretely made his way toward his own home. She looked after him as he was moving away and saw him open his house door and disappear. She did as he told her; she knocked, then stood waiting for the door to open.

She didn't have long to wait. The grandmother opened the door and led her inside. They entered a large, poorly lit room. The walls were whitewashed, in need of a fresh coat. The wooden floor was dark and rotting. A rickety old table and several chairs stood in the middle of the room. To the right of these furnishings there hung a curtain, concealing a partition that was the kitchen. It held a decrepit sink, stove and an old icebox. The wall facing them held a door leading to a small bedroom and bathroom. The door was closed and the grandmother, embracing her, spoke in a whisper:

"I'm so happy you're here at last, dear. Grandfather wanted to wait up for you, but he was exhausted. He hasn't been well lately." She hugged the girl with much warmth and tears moistening her round eyes. "You have been through a lot, haven't you, since we last saw each other?"

Sheinda responds with tears of her own. She hadn't realized how pent up her emotions had been. There had been constant need for control, for hiding her feelings, ever since she left them that day across the border. Had she missed the old people? There hadn't been much time to dwell on such sentiments. Now she let go and cried for a while, feeling relief when at last she was done.

"Have a bit of soup," the grandmother was saying, placing a bowl of liquid with potatoes and vegetables in it before her. A slice of dry bread and half an apple completed her meal. The girl hadn't eaten a thing since the half a slice of bread and some water for lunch and consumed the food in front of her with greed. When she was done with the meal and Grace the grandmother pointed her toward a cot that stood folded in a corner of the room. Together they opened it quietly, arranging the pillow and blanket the grandmother had brought from her bedroom. The girl said her prayers while the old lady stood watching; she then kissed the girl saying:

"Good Night then, I'll see you in the morning."

"Thank you, Bubtchu (diminutive for grandmother), good night."

She turned to the wall but was unable to fall asleep. Her journey, the anxiety it had involved, the prospect of reunion and what was awaiting them further — all that combined to keep her keyed up, alert, thinking.

The grandfather was ill, she had known it, of course. His various maladies were no news to her. In addition to his high blood pressure he suffered from diabetes, a troublesome combination. The two maladies combined to make him vulnerable to infection, which he was unable to rid himself of. Presently he suffered from large sores on his back, which didn't heal properly and had to be surgically cleaned. He was in great pain much of the time. Under normal circumstances they might have sought special attention for his medical problems. In these times, however, one's medical problems weren't given the attention they needed. No, it was better to lay low, not call attention to oneself. He did get insulin to cope with his diabetes. The grandmother gave him an injection every day.

I'll have to learn how to do it, to relieve the old lady once in a while, Sheinda was thinking; yes, I will do it, she resolved yawning. She turned around to face the wall again. For a long while she lay wide awake, her thoughts following one another in an endless chain until finally her body relaxed and she knew no more.

Among the families living in the same courtyard with the grandparents were people from many different regions, many of them refugees. Some of them, like the Weingarts, came from the eastern part of the state. Others, like the Sturms and Mayers, had always lived here, having their ancestors buried in the local cemetery. There were also many who had come to the city from across the border, where deportation of Jews was now in full swing. They had come to seek refuge here in this city where it was relatively safe at the moment. (With the exception of one transport there had been no deportations here in this state over the last two years.) The governing body and its policies had changed from radical to moderate. That fact, together with pressure from below, resulted in a degree of toleration (sufficiently so to relieve them of their money in the form of bribes) of the small number of Jews who had been left behind as necessary to the economy.)

The general population hadn't minded relieving Jews of their property and wealth; they had even condoned deportation. They could live without Jews, they felt, increasing their own opportunities for business and wealth. But many objected when rumors about the fate of the deported Jews began to reach them. Then there had been outcries against sending people to their deaths. Moreover, the German in charge of Jewish affairs at the moment was known to be "on the take." Hence the deportations had been halted, but not before two thirds of the Jewish population, including most young boys and girls aged sixteen and over, had been sent away; the young ones, to so called labor camps, which turned out to be death camps at a slower rate. They were allowed to work as long as their strength lasted, then were disposed of through starvation, illness or outright extermination, which had become the fate of all other European Jews unable to work. Few survived. These facts however were unknown to the young girl; they became clear to her only much later.)

She came to know several families whose households she is allowed to frequent. The Weingarts were among those she liked best. Mr. Weingart, a ritual slaughterer back home, is a man of some prominence well versed in the Talmud and other Judaica. He is a tall, well-built individual with a round face and ruddy complexion. His blond beard is full, without any grey in it; his side curls tidy, arranged in two neat coils that hug his face. He is a friendly man with smiling, brown eyes, welcoming her warmly whenever she appears in their abode.

Mrs. Weingart, also an attractive lady of some physical stature, has about her the manner of the teacher. That was her occupation back home, that is, but she continues to practice her vocation in unofficial capacity. Sheinda is the beneficiary of much Mrs. Weingart has to impart, dealing as often as not with local, residential matters and with relationships within the courtyard they share. She listens attentively to the advice being offered her.

Her main attraction at the Weingart household is their young daughter Surale. She is a hefty girl of about seventeen, statuesque and healthy-looking like her parents. Her features are good: the nose is straight, the mouth small, her brown hair glossy and she has a warm smile. Yet together they add up to what is commonly referred to as comely, rather than beautiful. Surale is not one to be concerned with her looks though. She is a jolly sort, has taken her young friend under her wing and together they explore the surrounding neighborhood as well as the outlying areas of the city.

Surale has a wonderful grasp of the city: its layout, its important buildings, parks, gardens and markets. The two girls spend much time walking around exploring these various places: one in the role of teacher, the other her eager pupil. The place they like best is the Promenade, a boardwalk along the Danube where, in good weather, there are always people streaming by: some at an energetic pace, engaged in their daily exercise, others at a leisurely gait taking an afternoon or evening stroll. The two of them like to sit on a bench under one of the trees lining the riverbank, a front row seat over the spectacle unfolding before them. The expanse of blue water before them is immense, stretching as far across as the eye can see and disappearing into the horizon. On the boardwalk behind them, they can see people from all walks of life and of all ages: the young, the old and the children, drawn by the enormous river like a sea before them. The girls, of course, must be circumspect. They cannot reveal their identity.

One afternoon, as the two girls are sitting on one of these benches, they are joined by a tall young woman who takes up the other end of their bench. She appears to be a woman in her late twenties: a pleasant blue eyed blond. She is very polite; she introduces herself, smiles at them and asks:

"Do you mind if I sit here a while? I'm out of breath. I walked further than I intended to."

The girls are taken aback. Discretion has long been one of their prime rules. Avoid disclosure and entanglements is the unspoken commandment they have come to accept as a matter of course. They look at each other for a brief moment, then rise, as if by agreement, and are ready to resume their walk, when the young woman stops them.

"Wait! Don't go yet!" the latter calls out suddenly. "I want to know your names; I told you mine, remember?" Indeed, she had; she told them her name was Berta and that she worked at the art studio above the bakery on Gate street.

"I know where that is!" Surale exclaims. "I'll show you the spot," she says, turning to her young friend. Then she addressed their new acquaintance again:

"I know someone who works in the bakery over there. I go there often. May we stop and visit you sometimes when we're there?"

"Yes, of course, I hope you come soon!" says Berta, "I want us to get to know each other, to become friends, if you don't mind having an old woman like me for a friend, that is." The girls laugh.

"Have you always lived here, in this city, I mean?" Surale asks.

"I've been here for a long time," the young woman replies, she says no more, but smiles encouragingly. There is something

135

about her — what is it? warmth? kindness? a message of goodwill; a desire to connect?

"My name is Sara Weingarten, and this is my friend Anny who lives next door to us, Surale says, moving a step closer to Berta.

Surale uses her own version of diminutive for Anna (of which Anča is another) as she points to her young friend and the latter is pleased. She likes the sound of Anny: it is novel, and it carries none of the negatives she came to associate with Anča. It gives her importance; a new personality. She takes a step toward Berta and, finding her own voice, says:

"It was nice meeting you. We hope to see you again soon."

"Yes, do come," replies Berta "I hope you both come to see me soon! Good bye."

"So long," the girls chant in unison as they leave to return home.

Sheinda spent a fairly pleasant few weeks with her grandparents here in this city and with the new friends she had made, among whom Berta came to occupy an increasingly prominent place. Berta, aware of the great naiveté of the girl, stepped into the role of her guide. She needed protection, Berta thought, a bit of planning ahead in preparation for what was to come. Berta herself felt secure in her job. She knew her work was important, sought after, and that even if the community (the Jews) were soon to be dispersed, as rumors persisted that it will, she, Berta, will be able to remain where she is.

For some time now Berta not only worked in the shop above the bakery, she also lived there. Unbeknownst to her co-workers, including her employer, she managed to bring over and hide a few basic necessities. The studio had several storage areas in one of which there was a sink, a little stove and cupboard space. Berta's employer, pleased with her resourcefulness, asked no questions. She knew that Berta must work after hours to keep up with her load, since much of her time was spent supervising the work of others. She found it logical that Berta should be the first one there and the last one to leave and saw to it that Berta had her own key. She knew she could trust Berta.

"Why, I could leave gold about the place; I trust her absolutely," Mrs. Čačka, Berta's employer, proclaimed to her husband. "And what a worker! A pair of golden hands she has. I don't know what I would do without her. Everyone clamors for her workmanship and she helps me with the others, too. Why, she practically runs the place. I suppose I will have to make it official soon; give her the title of manager and a raise to go with it. She certainly deserves it."

Berta never removed her old address from the books, so there was an official residence where she supposedly repaired to each night If anyone suspected otherwise, they didn't show it: there were no signs that anyone suspected however.

Several times now the young girl had been to visit Berta in her shop. She came to love and admire everything about her: her dexterity, her kindness, her charm and dignity. Berta was a strong person: she knew who she was and what she wanted. She would amuse the girl with stories about her life: her town, her family and friends, their common tradition and above all, the man she was engaged to.

"He is a distant relative of mine," Berta had told her when she inquired about his identity. "Here, look at his picture; isn't he handsome?"

"Yes, he is," the girl replied, holding the slightly creased photo, which was beginning to turn at the edges. It had evidently been much used, probably carried about wherever Berta went. The image was of a tall young man clad in black garb with a reddish beard and sideburns. He had a pleasant enough face with strong, even features and he was smiling. Still, Sheinda was disappointed. She had expected someone more imposing for the woman she had come to admire so. As if reading her mind, Berta added:

"Of course, it isn't his looks only — or even primarily. It's his personality. You have to know him to understand what he is really like. There simply aren't any words to describe him: his wonderful gentle nature, not to mention his intellect. He is s-o-o brilliant, and his sense of humor is incredible! He makes me laugh, you see? That's what I like most about him, the way he makes me laugh."

"I can see you like him a lot. Does he feel the same way about you?"

"I believe so," Berta smiled. "He makes me feel very good, as though I am the most important person in the world."

"I should hope so," the girl said. "You're admired by all who know you and he is expected to marry you, to be your chosen one, I mean for the rest of your life!"

"I hope so, if God wills it. The main thing now is to hold out until we can be together again."

"Where is he?" the girl asked.

"Where all the other young Jewish men are: in some labor camp digging ditches for the soldiers. But he will return. I know he will, he must, we promised each other to endure; to find one another after it's all over. I live in this faith; it is this hope that keeps me going. I could scarcely exist otherwise."

"Yes, he must," Sheinda said. "I wish you luck." She was glad her friend had such a central purpose to hang on to. But what if the young man didn't return...? The thought flashed through her mind but she dismissed it at once, unwilling to contemplate such possibility.

On one such visit Berta took her young friend down to the bakery and introduced her to an acquaintance.

"Rozsika, I want you to meet a young friend of mine," she told the middle aged woman behind the counter. The woman looked up from her work, then approached the girl and shook hands with her warmly.

"Glad to meet you," she said smiling, then returned to her place in the store.

Rozsika was short and squat with thick, shiny black hair and plain features. Her dress looked drab; her shoes were worn and turning at the heels, but her eyes were warm, welcoming and put the girl at ease.

"Rozsika is very good to me," Berta explained. "She and I manage to spend a bit of time together now and then, don't we, Rozsika?"

"Indeed, we do," replied the woman. "Berta furnishes the coffee and I, the rolls, and we have fun talking. Why don't you two stick around for a while? I'll be taking my break soon and we can show your young friend what we mean instead of just talking about it?"

The girls agreed and the three of them soon met in the little room behind the store that was part of the bakery premises. The room was dark, without a window, but it was furnished with a table and chairs as well as a cupboard with plates, cups and other kitchen utensils. A small gas range stood against one of the walls with a kettle of boiling water on it. Evidently Rozsika kept a pot of boiling water ready for just such a contingency.

"Sit down! Make yourselves at home!" she commanded cheerily. "If you want, you can set out the cups and plates while I bring the rolls. There is sugar in the cupboard and Berta knows where we hide her coffee, don't you, Berta?" She smiled mischievously and hurried out to bring the food.

The girls laughed a good deal during their repast. They were encouraged to visit frequently and they did, shooting the breeze with Rozika who always managed to make it a pleasant experience. The girl, though she knew little of the woman's personal life, came to think of Rozika as a friend on whom she could rely. It was good that she had friends like these, she thought, but little did she know how desperately she will soon need them. "Ya-fa! Ya-fa!" It is the grandmother calling, using the girl's Hebrew code name: the name her parents have used in correspondence and her grandparents when addressing her in public.

"I'm co-ming!" Sheinda calls back from the yard where she has been talking to her friend Surale Weingart. They are both worried: for some time now the families in their yard, those who lived here in this haven, have been dispersing. It's certain now: the transports to Poland are to begin again, the protection Jews have enjoyed for the last two years here is at an end.

It is the fall of 1944. There has been intense partisan activity in the central region of the state precipitating an uprising among the population there. The Germans no longer rely on their recalcitrant ally to quash the rebellion; they send their own troops into the state. They deal with the rebels in their proven gruesome manner, then go after the Jews.

The remnants of the Jewish community are desperate: consultations are going on within the ghetto: in study houses, the synagogue, the market, in shops, streets and in private dwellings. What to do? All agree that sitting and waiting isn't good, but only the lucky few, those who have the wherewithal and a bit of luck, manage to get away. They have made connections, have put away money and suddenly disappear. Where to? Where are they going?

No one is sure. They may be going into hiding locally, or perhaps attempt to cross the border once again, running, without knowing where. Perhaps they are acting on the rumor that Hungary is defying the Germans and are determined to cross borders in the hope of getting there.

The grandfather, being the scion of an exalted rabbinic dynasty and a Hasidic rabbi himself, is able to find a place to hide. It is provided by a group of young single men who, with the assistance of a non-Jewish acquaintance, had obtained a bunker, a hiding place, for themselves. When first approached, they had refused: it was inconceivable that they would make room for an old Hasidic rabbi, Hasidism had been somewhat remote from their Westernized, Jewish life-style; especially so to Janko, the man whose initiative had made it all possible: he was not even a practicing Jew. The grandfather, however, was willing to provide them with something they did not have: a guarantee that should they make room for him, their venture would meet with success. Not even Janko was able to resist such a promise. He was sufficiently superstitious, if no longer religious, to believe in the necessity of placating the evil forces:

"Who knows, perhaps this rabbi does have some extraordinary powers and will manage to keep us all secure? The old fellow certainly seems to believe so himself. He is so confident; his promise so ironclad: a virtual guarantee. It would give us this extra bit of hope, don't you see?"

Thus argues Janko and so it is that the grandfather leaves them one sunny morning. There is no room for either the grandmother, the rabbi's wife, or the young girl, his granddaughter, in the bunker. Sheinda doesn't know what the grandfather's intentions are: does he hope to make room for them by and by? Does he simply accept the inevitable; the rationale that to save one is better than to save none? He didn't say. There is no time to ponder, however. It is necessary to act and so she decides to join a group of people who are making their way across the border once again.

She says a hurried goodbye to all her friends and finally to the grandmother who is walking back and forth in the little kitchen saying her morning prayers, as usual. If she feels anxious, or abandoned, the grandmother doesn't show it. She hugs the girl

140

quietly, shedding a few tears as she does so and the latter hurries away to once again seek her separate fortune.

She is with a group of people — about a dozen altogether. There are a few couples: young married people without any children. "What happened to the children?" she wonders. "Well, let's hope there were no children; it's not impossible." It's also possible, as she well knows, that these people left their children behind somewhere. Who knows? Some couples in the group are engaged, or to be so soon. The rest are single people like herself. One young man, Avrum, is on his way to rejoin his relatives across the border. He is the one who takes charge of her:

"I promised your grandparents to look after you," he explains and she is glad. It's good to have someone in charge; someone to point the way for you.

"At least I won't be alone when sudden decisions are called for," she reflects, and the thought lifts some of the weight off her shoulders.

They are assembled at the railroad station. They have purchased the tickets and are waiting for their train to pull in. This time there is no guide in charge. The plan, very hurriedly put together, is for them to be on their own while on the train; they will then assemble at the last station before the border and will proceed together from there.

Avrum, a slender youth of medium height with dark hair and alert intelligent eyes, stands, immersed in thought, observing the scene before him. Sheinda looks in the same direction and sees the street across from the station with its neat houses surrounded by gardens still vibrant with shrubs and flowers, the people in the street rushing back and forth. Some of them are headed in their direction, and they soon make their way to the ticket booth.) In the distance, bluish hills are visible, illuminate by bright sunlight now that the last shreds of the morning mist have lifted. It will be a lovely day. But Avrum seems troubled. He looks around furtively, takes several sudden strides toward one of the couples as if to accost them, then turns away and starts a restless pacing.

The girl looks around her uneasily and begins to comprehend. Too many in their group stand out from the rank and file passengers around them: their dress, their manner, their excess baggage, their sad, concerned faces, all this sets them apart. They look out of place and are likely to arouse suspicion. (She can't help being reminded of that other fateful train ride during which everyone except she and her then companion, the rabbi's son, were caught and taken off the train.)

"This is a bad spot to be in," says Avrum, turning to the girl. "Let's get away from here, and — " he has no time to finish his sentence. Suddenly, a lorry pulls up near the platform. A group of gendarmes jump out and surround the passengers. They quickly isolate the refugees, herd them into the waiting vehicle and carry them off to the local jail. The refugees spend the night and all of the next day in detention. After they have conceded their Jewish identity their captors make preparations to send them back to the city.

"These people do not belong here — we have our own Jews to deal with — it's best to send them back. Let the locality they come from deal with them!" So goes the argument.

The prisoners appoint a spokesman and with the help of a substantial bribe, their captors agree to let them loose rather than deliver them into the hands of the authorities. Most of the group are satisfied with that arrangement: They accept their failure as an accomplished fact and are willing to return. Not so Avrum. He perceives the opportunity to try again — to put his original plan of escape into action once more. As soon as their captors have deposited them in the agreed upon spot and left, he approaches the others with his plan, but they rebuff him. No one is willing to try again. No — they want to return and take their place in the ranks of their brethren. They won't try again!

Avrum argues with them, but in vain. He finally turns away in disgust. "Where do they think they're going, the idiots?" he mumbles, returning to Sheinda — the only one who will listen to his counsel.

"'We shall return," he mimics. "Look at them! They're actually excited about going back. They think they're going to some adventure, to have a ball! I'll tell you where they're going — to the concentration camps in Poland, that's where. They'll be sent away, every one of them, but I will not be among them if I can help it!"

So said Avrum, her self-appointed protector, and Sheinda is in no position to refute him. Indeed, her own assessment tells her that he is probably right. The situation back in the city is not good.

"I suggest that you join me if you want to get away. I don't know where we shall turn, but whatever we do, we probably stand a better chance, the two of us, on our own. I suggest we move now, without much explanation."

"I agree," the girl whispers, realizing that she must trust and follow him. He is the only other human being she now has to rely on and it's much better than being alone.

"Thanks!" she says. "Yes, I will come with you." They inform the others of their decision and quickly leave the scene.

It is late in the afternoon on that same day. They have put countless miles behind them. The sun has not yet set, but it soon will. When it does, they will still have to wait for the remnants of daylight to disappear. Only then, hidden by the mantle of dark, will it be safe for them to venture into the streets leading to the railroad station in this town they now find themselves in. They had apparently made it across the border, judging by the store signs and language used here by the locals. They have been wandering around here in the square of this little town for the better part of an hour. They ventured into an eatery, obtained a couple of pieces of stale bread and some milk laced with water. They swallowed the food hurriedly giving the appearance of people in a rush not to miss the train.

In the street once again, they looked about anxiously, striding with purpose as if they had someplace definite to go. Such, of course, was not the case. They were at a complete loss where to go — where to find some bit of space that would shelter and hide them from view. They knew they must get out of sight of people.

They could find no such place however and resigned themselves to sit down on a bench in front of a store, when the girl spotted what must have been an abandoned kiosk along the sidewalk a few paces away. It looked as though it hadn't been in use for some time, but still had the walls and roof intact. They entered it and saw with relief that it still held the counter, behind which was a hollowed out space that might have once held some shelves. They crawled into that narrow space, put their bags between them and sat down to wait.

They were sheltered from view now. This was certainly better than a bench in the street, but the place was too public for real repose: they were in the middle of a busy square; could hear the clang and bustle — the noises of a busy little town with a railroad juncture. They were unable to sleep here. That fact may have been fatal; it lead them into action that was unwise. Toward evening they had become very restless. Hunger and thirst contributed to their decision to abandon the shelter before it was quite dark and to wander through the streets in search of food.

They were successful in obtaining something to eat: In a coffee shop they ordered and consumed slices of the local black bread with margarine and glasses of something that resembled hot chocolate. They also asked for and obtained directions to the train station at the other end of town. They had gone only a few steps from the coffee shop, however, when they were accosted and detained. Someone had informed the authorities.

They are in jail! It is a little room adjacent to the police station of the locality in which they were caught. They are sitting on the cold earthen floor of the bare cell, huddled together for warmth. Their soiled damp clothes cling to their frozen bodies, but they care little about that; they are much too dejected and worried.

"What are they going to do to us?" the girl asks quietly, addressing herself to her companion. "Is there anything we can do; ought to do, I mean?"

"Yes, there is," replies Avrum. "Definitely! We must create a doubt in them as to our identity."

"How are we going to do that? Didn't they bring us here because they know we are Jews running from our fate?"

"No!" Avrum replies emphatically. "They don't know that! They suspect, yes, but that isn't the same as knowing; as having evidence. We have documents to show that we are Polish Gentiles on our way to the metropolis where we shall be under the protection of the Polish Consul. All we have to do is to keep stressing that, remaining firm: this is who we are and we must remain consistent with that claim. As long as we stick to our story we may succeed. They have nothing to prove that we are Jews.

We, however, must give some evidence of being Gentiles. The first thing you must do, for instance, is learn to recite the Lord's

Prayer in Polish. This is something every Christian is supposed to know and it would help us convince them."

"But how am I to learn the Lord's Prayer in Polish?"

"From me — I'll teach you. It's the first thing I did when I decided to pose as a Polish Gentile."

So that's how it was. Under Avrum's patient tutelage, she learned to recite the Lord's Prayer in Polish until she knew it fluently. Throughout the interrogations, which seemed interminable — first together, then in separate rooms in an attempt to trip them up, to create discrepancies in their story — she had the opportunity to recite it as evidence of her assumed identity. The two of them remained firm. Thanks to Avrum who had given her courage, she was able to keep to her part of it. She didn't know what went on in the other room, but knew that he would stick to their version through every type of pressure and it was up to her to back him up. Luckily, the officials here had no specific policy to follow: no deportation was going on here at the moment and their action seemed geared to protecting themselves, to cover their tracks rather than persecute their captives.

Since they lacked specific instructions about what to do with the two of them, their captors were willing to make the following deal with them: they would take them to the border and release them, provided that they return to the state beyond the border — the one they came from. Having agreed to that provision, their captors told them to prepare for departure in the morning.

The next day dawned crisp and clear. It was still dark outside, but they were ready, sitting near the door next to which stood their bags to be taken up at a moment's notice, when they heard brisk footsteps: someone was approaching and came to a halt in front of the door. A moment later the door opened to reveal a man dressed in military garb, with a gun hanging from the leather strap around his waist. He stood a moment in the doorway, then entered, looked them over, and said, "You're the prisoners to be taken to the border, then?" The comment was more confirmation than query, requiring no reply and they gave none.

"Will you be taking us there?" the girl inquired.

"Yes, but — not yet!" he added, as if in afterthought. "Before we can do so we must check some details in your documents. Come with me now!" he commanded.

The two of them picked up their packs and followed him out. He led them across the yard into the main compound housing the offices of the police. He opened the door and took them through a long, narrow corridor toward the other end of the building. Here he stopped in front of a door, which he opened, revealing a staircase leading to the cellar. He entered the staircase and as the two of them were about to follow suit he turned and held out his hand barring the approach of Avrum. "You wait up here!" he ordered and placing a firm hand on the girl's shoulder and pulling her along said: "You come with me!"

She panicked. Why is he taking her down there by herself? What does he want with her? She lost control and began to cry, shouting hysterically:

"No! no, I will not! I won't go down there with you! Let go of me!" She repeated her entreaties several times as she wriggled out from under his grasp.

Her outcries were loud enough to bring out several other officials in the building who wanted to know what the commotion was all about. After conferring with them for awhile, his fellow officials left the scene leaving the officer who had brought them in charge once again.

The girl in the meantime had managed to bring her hysteria under control. She began pleading with the officer, speaking quietly now, but emphatically, in an appeal to his emotions — his humanity:

"Perhaps you meant no harm, but I am scared, don't you see? Put yourself in my position. Suppose I were your sister — would you like it if some strange man with a gun forced me down a cellar? — "

"But I only want to question you — I will do you no harm — " he insisted, with a smile he was trying to conceal.

"You can question me up here, I'll give you all the information you need. Please!" she pleaded.

Whatever his original intent, the officer gave up. He gestured with his hand, dismissing her curtly. He did take them into an adjoining office, questioning them briefly, after which he drove them to a certain juncture of a nearby road and pointed out the direction they must take. He cautioned:

"See that you cross over to the other side. If you ever show up here again, we'll have to shoot you!" He turned around and left.

In line with his character and his custom during their recent experiences together, Avrum began insisting almost at once that they try again. No sooner had the officer left them in the field, than Avrum began insisting that they continue their quest to reach the metropolis. He simply saw no point in returning to the city they had come from. They will simply reverse the direction their guide had pointed them in, he argued, and will inevitably arrive at some station, some locality with a train to the interior of this state where they wanted to go. This is a new chance, he insisted, an opportunity they simply cannot afford to ignore.

Sheinda had neither the stamina nor the inclination to argue. Somewhere in her consciousness there lurked the fear that they might be caught again, but the same danger existed for them wherever they went, that much she had to concede. And so it was that they simply turned around and continued their journey with a glimmer of renewed hope.

They must now tread carefully: they could not afford to be apprehended again. They slowly made their way into the dense forest that ringed this town on its southern end. This was the right direction, the one they needed, but there were no clear paths within the forest and no signs to mark their progress out of it. They could only hope, as they groped about in the dark, that the narrow path they were following was the right one.

It was only the beginning of fall and the day had been warm, filled with sunshine. But the night now was cold and it was beginning to rain. The raindrops came scantily at first, and Sheinda and her companion were shielded by the thickness of the forest. Soon, however, the drops changed to a downpour, then to a torrent. The water came rushing at them from every side in a steady stream until they were drenched to their bones. Everything they had on them was dripping water; they were soaked and shivering from the wetness and cold. The boy approached a tree and removed his pack:

"We aren't going to make much progress while it's raining so hard," he explained, "we might as well stop for a while. It's the Eve of *Sukkoth*, you know; I've been saying the prayers, all I could remember by heart. I will say the *Amidah* now, then we will continue."

147

"Good," replied the girl, following her friend into the shelter of the tree. She situated herself a few paces away, so as to have a view from which to observe him.

The tree didn't provide much shelter. Its branches and leaves were filled with water that flowed unto their heads. It no longer mattered, however; they were soaked through already.

The girl now stood with her back against the trunk and watched her companion in silence.

Avrum stood with his face turned up toward the sky, his eyes closed. His hands in his *gartel* (a silken black belt used for prayer by males) circling his waist, he swayed back and forth, while chanting the prayer silently. The girl admired his presence of mind and his devotion. She had forgotten — hadn't remembered what day it was.

At home, under normal circumstances, he would be in the synagogue praying with other male congregants. She, being a female, would not be required to be at the synagogue for the evening service; she would recite her prayers at her festively decked out home and, in the company of other females, all beautifully dressed for the occasion, would await the return of the men.

How well she remembered the delights of that holiday, including the building and decorating of the *Sukkah* [tabernacle, or tent], accomplished with the help of every family member able to render it, amidst much bustle and joy. But now, what circumstances are these? How is it possible? The two of them so alone, lost here in this forest...in the middle of this dreadful night: running for their lives...yes, their lives! And no one cares!?

As she observed Avrum she too wanted to pray, but hadn't mastered the prayer; she didn't know it by heart. She closed her eyes, which were filling up with tears and murmured silently:

"Dear God, on this holy day, please help us! Help us find our way and lead us to safety."

She then sat on the ground, her back against the tree, her head on her knees and sobbed, silently and long. Her tears brought relief. She slowly raised her head, dried her eyes and stood up. Her companion had finished his prayer by then; they resumed their journey through the dark.

They wandered the entire night, with only a glimmer of an idea as to the direction they ought to follow. They fared better by morning. Somehow, by observing the location and progress of the sun through the sky, they were able to determine the path leading south and that was the direction they followed. They finally managed to make it out of the forest and at once began looking for shelter. They must find shelter again until dark, for it was now broad daylight and it wouldn't do to be detected by nearby villagers.

They walked to the nearest settlement, a cluster of farmhouses and hid in the barn of the first one they could reach. The approach had been risky; they could have encountered people and dogs, but luck was with them: there was nothing to impede their way and they sat quietly in the barn behind a large bale of hay. They searched through their bags and found a few stale raisins and nuts, very likely the only food they will have that day. They ate, then settled down to rest.

It was evening when they awoke. They had fallen asleep instantly and slept undisturbed all this time. How lucky for them that the household in whose barn they found themselves were apparently away. Nothing else would explain the fact that there was no movement or noise of any sort coming from the house. They didn't wait to ponder the circumstances but resolved to leave at once, as long as they had the chance to do so.

After a prolonged trek through meadows and woods, beset by hunger and thirst, they arrived in what appeared to be a substantial town. Their first thought was to stop and eat somewhere, but they rejected it as too risky. They would work their way toward the railroad station first. Surely there was some train going through here? There must be in a town this size, but how to get to it? They must ask someone without arousing suspicion.

They sat on a bench under a tree near what appeared to be a schoolhouse. The building seemed deserted, but in one corner of it there was light coming from one of its windows. Should they knock and inquire? They decided against that. They'll wait — someone would surely turn up whom they could ask.

They sat and waited, but nothing happened. The hour was late and the location, a side street, was out of the way and deserted. No one was coming or going by.

"Let's walk for a bit. I'm cold and my legs are getting numb. Nobody will see us in this forsaken place — what do you think?"

Sheinda rose before she finished speaking, put her arms above her head and stretched. She looked relieved and waited for a response.

"Let's give it another half hour before going anywhere. If nothing happens during that time, we'll take some action. We'll have to, for it's getting late, we mustn't miss the opportunity to get on a train soon. You can walk up and down this street for a bit, but don't go too far."

After an interval of about an hour, longer than they had intended, they decided that it was time to go. They had no idea which way to turn, so they just began walking, intending to retrace their steps into the direction they had come from. They had gone only a few paces, when they heard voices approaching from the vicinity of the schoolhouse. They stopped and waited. There was nowhere to hide, nothing to conceal them, anyway. They would have to take the chance, confront these people, whoever they were and get the information they needed.

Presently the people they had heard came into view. They were a group consisting of several men and two women. They carried buckets, brooms and other equipment on their arms and shoulders: a cleaning crew on their way home, having finished their job at the school, apparently. This was their chance. Safe or not, the two of them approached and without further hesitation the girl asked:

"Could you please tell us the way to the railroad station? We must leave on the next train out of here."

"Must you?" the elder of the women said with a dubious smile, looking at them uneasily. "You're running away from home then, are you? Well, you'll get caught soon enough, won't you? As soon as your money runs out. No need for us to fret about it."

"No, no! we don't live here! We're passing through here, on our way home. We're strangers here, this is why we need you to show us the way, don't you see?"

"Oh, I see! You're from one of the nearby villages then?"

"No!" said Avrum and left it at that. He was afraid to explain. The less said, the better, he thought.

"Look, we don't have time to give you the details. It's late, could you please show us the way? We'll be very grateful," he implored.

The woman stood there looking at them for a long while. She spoke no more and gave no hint of what she might be thinking. She then looked at her companions — each one in turn. Finally, she turned to the two of them and said abruptly:

"Alright, why don't you just follow me for a while, then." She dismissed the others in her crew:

"Good night to you all, I'll see you tomorrow, hey?" She hurried along, motioning for the girl and her friend to follow.

She took them through a long street in what looked like the center of town. From there through several side streets, until they were in a different section, or suburb. Here she pointed them toward a long street, the end of which lay in the far distance. She instructed:

"Just follow this street toward its end. Don't go either right, or left, just straight ahead until you have almost reached the end of the street and you'll see the station on your left. It's a large, gray building. The railroad tracks are in back of it. Good night, then, and good luck!" She turned and left them alone, before they had a chance to thank her.

They entered through the doors and found themselves in a large waiting area. In spite of the lateness of the hour, there were many passengers assembled here. Some were waiting their turn in front of the ticket booth, others, their business already concluded, were sitting with their luggage piled near their seats. Some were scanning the bulletin board for the times of departure and arrival.

The young girl and her companion sat down on an empty bench near a door leading to one of the tracks and surveyed the situation.

"This is quite a large station," remarked Avrum. "There must be trains coming and going, judging by the number of people here. We must proceed with speed. The first thing I suggest is that we freshen up a bit. Then, let's meet out here again and go buy our tickets.

"Good," Sheinda agreed. "I'm hungry, as well. I think it's safe to go into that booth over there," she pointed, "to get a bite. What do you think? I need a glass of milk very badly."

"Maybe a good idea, but I would like to secure our tickets first. Hurry up, don't take longer than a few minutes, we'll have time to relax on the train."

They both left in search of the washrooms.

They are finally on the train: the compartment they are in is crammed with people. Nevertheless, they each have a seat. They want to sink into obscurity now, to hide behind closed lids; perhaps to sleep a bit. The girl shuts her eyes and tries to relax. It hadn't been easy to come to this point. They had managed to get something to eat in the station. They purchased the tickets for the metropolis with money used in this state, which Avrum had kept hidden in an invisible pocket of his coat. The rest of their money the authorities had taken.

The last minutes in the waiting room and through the gate toward the trains had been filled with confusion and anxiety. Two trains stood facing each other on either side of the platform, headed for different destinations. They didn't known which train was theirs and had to wait until the last minute before they got the information. They almost missed getting on, it was a close call. But, here they are at last, headed for the metropolis once again.

The documents showing them to be Polish citizens of Gentile stock was the only thing that they needed now, in case they are required to identify themselves. Fortunately, the prison officials had returned the documents. What Sheinda now wanted was a good long rest, free of worry, and some sleep. She pulled her legs up on the seat, tucking them in to the left of her. She pressed the length of her back against her seat, hunched her shoulders, allowing her head to drop to one side and pulled her old, threadbare blanket tightly around her. She will sink into oblivion, will look at no one and hopefully no one will notice her.

...They are on the platform running frantically after the train...it's their train, the last one out of the station, but it's beyond their reach; it's moving ever so slowly and they run, reaching the compartment door just in time, but before they manage to get on, it suddenly moves out of their reach. "Stop! Stop the train!" the frantic call breaks involuntarily from the girl's lips and falls on dead silence. They watch helplessly as the train disappears out of sight....

"Don't worry dear, I will find us another train soon." It's her brother Chaim talking. His hand is on her shoulder and he smiles at her encouragingly. He hasn't changed. His eyes are deep-set and blue, his lashes thick and golden, and he is tall, taller than she remembers him. But what is that noise? Why is he shaking her and

calling out: "Wake up! It's time to wake up!" She smiles at him and opens her eyes.

Avrum has her by the shoulder and is talking to her. By his side, but facing the other way, stands the train conductor with the tickets in one hand and the rest of the paraphernalia of his trade in the other. He has seemingly concluded checking theirs, for he moves on, leaving them together.

"We're on the wrong train!" Avrum whispers to her and sits down, dejected, in the empty seat facing her. He leans forward to make it possible to continue to converse inaudibly.

"I think it's meant to be, it's fated! In spite of all we tried, we are headed back to the city...You see, we got on the wrong train after all. We are not headed into the interior, toward the metropolis. We are back across the border."

"But our documents — "

"I know! It's a miracle! The official at the border examined them and waved us on, just like that, can you imagine? Well, it's destiny...there is nothing we can do; we'll have to disembark soon. You slept for a long time."

"What about the tickets? We have the wrong ones, don't we?"

"Yes, but the conductor exchanged them. There was some difference in price: the ones he gave me cost less, so I told him to keep the change."

"So, we're returning to the City...!" the girl leaned back in her seat reflecting, coming to terms with the significance of the new situation. Where will she go? To whom will she turn now? He, Avrum, will try again, no doubt. His mind was made up, and who knows, maybe he will succeed in the end. But not she! She had enough. She will seek her fortune in the City. She did have friends there — some of them may still be there, within reach. She will see... first she must see her way out of this train and into the streets safely.

They got off at a suburban stop eager to avoid the main city station. This meant a considerable walk, but greater safety. As they entered the road leading toward the neighborhood they were most familiar with, they stopped briefly to say goodbye. They both understood that they must part ways now.

"What will you do? Do you have somewhere to go?" she asked with concern in her voice.

"I'll try again eventually," he answered "after I contact some people and make arrangements. Yes, I know where I'm going. What about you?"

"I'll try some of my friends....Look, we better be on our way while it's still dark. Goodbye, Avrum, and thanks for all your help!" She turned away and began walking rapidly down the street.

She ought to be used to it by now, the sudden need to say goodbye to people she had come to depend on. But she is sad, so sad...she wants to sit down somewhere, bury her head and cry. It's different now! She finally admits to herself, coming to a sudden stop. "There is more to it now, isn't there? This time — it hurts more somehow. We have been through so much together, the two of us — I leaned on him...he gave me support. Did I also grow too fond of him and don't really want to see him go?" She stands awhile, forlorn, leaning against a wall and allows the pangs of regret to wash over her. She cries, but only for a while: she soon composes herself and wipes away the thick tears that had fallen on her cheeks. She sighs, and slowly resumes her walk. Like it or not, she must now begin a new segment in the fight for her survival and she must do it all alone.

CHAPTER THIRTEEN
BACK IN THE CITY

She pulled herself together and began walking toward her destination. She will not go home (to the apartment she had shared with her grandparents in this city), there would be no point. The grandfather was in a shelter somewhere in the mountains that surrounded the city — a bunker of sorts. She knew no more than that. She didn't know where the grandmother was. What she did know was that at this point in time, she would be looking in vain for Jews with legal residence in the city. Whoever is left here lives either in hiding or in some other concealed manner. She must do the same.

She knew her friend Berta lived in the city; more important, she knew where Berta lived: still in the studio above the bakery. One day, shortly before she left, Berta had said to her: "I'll always be here, you know? So, if you need me, you know where to find me." She stopped to think about it. Should she try Berta? No, she decided after a few minutes' reflection: she'll try some other way. She'll leave Berta alone for now. Gejza — the thought popped into her head suddenly — what about him and his friends? That might be an idea: she could certainly use that kind of help, yes, she will try him. She had never actually seen Gejza, only heard about what he and a few others were planning: They were going to provide documents for people (Jews) willing to risk living in the city under assumed identities, like she will now have to do.

There was a problem with this plan: she didn't have his address, didn't know where he lived, and it wouldn't do her any good if she did: how could she go, at this hour, knocking on the door of a man she didn't know?

She stood there, dismayed, reluctant to give up on this possibility when..."wait a minute," she told herself with a glimmer of renewed hope: "wasn't there some address I heard about on the day before we left? Something about an underground office in a basement somewhere...? What was it? Let me see — we weren't supposed to write it down, just memorize it. It was — number fifteen! Yes, fifteen, I'm sure of it! But where? What's the name of the street?" She stood racking her brain but was unable to recall it. "Problem is I didn't try hard enough; didn't think I will ever need it: I was going away, after all, wasn't I?"

A painful sigh akin to a sob broke from deep within her: She gave up dejectedly and began walking without aim, in disgust with herself, not knowing whither to turn.

She had been walking for a few minutes only when she suddenly stopped: Železnicka! the name of the street — yes, yes, that was it! It had suddenly appeared, rising to the surface of her consciousness. "I have it!" she exclaimed in exultation, but immediately reasserted outward control. Her inner elation continued, however: Not only did she have the name now, she also remembered the street and knew the way there.

She resumed her walk, but her demeanor had changed: she walked in the manner of one who knew her destination. She soon arrived in the street she wanted and located number fifteen, the building she needed. She stopped before the doorway and looked around.

It was very early in the morning, around five o'clock, she judged. The new day was barely breaking: the shadows of the night lingered still, but soon their protective mantle will be lifted to be succeeded by the glow of the morning light. Already she could hear in the distance the signals of the approaching day: the roar of an engine, the barking of dogs, the noisy clatter of a shutting gate, the fall of footsteps on the pavement. It's time to go in! she decided.

She made her entrance very quietly, grateful that the door had opened as she tried the handle, and found herself in a small vestibule. The door facing her led to a narrow hallway at the side of which was another door. She opened this door, careful to prevent creaking and found what she was looking for: the staircase to the basement. She descended the steps and remained standing where she was, on the landing. Facing her was a door to a tiny storage area — perhaps a pantry once: the door stood open; there were shelves lining one wall here holding much household clutter. To her left was a large room that looked like a lounge. In the center of it stood a table surrounded by chairs. The wall facing the entrance held the windows and a fireplace of sorts. There was a sofa — perhaps concealing a bed — along one wall and several old armchairs stood arranged near the corners of the room.

To the right (of the landing) was another large area that looked like a laundry. At the far end of this room — beneath tiny windows placed high on the wall — stood a large washbasin with faucets leading out of a pipe behind it. There was a coal furnace in this room and a storage bin for the coal in a small room facing the furnace. Off to the right — behind the furnace — there was another, partially hidden door. The girl approached and tried this door: it was locked. She moved away and looked around the room in search of somewhere to sit. At last she chose the corner between the basin and the furnace — the corner to the right of the closed door — and sat down to wait. She was hungry and had nothing to eat, but the room was warm. She was exhausted and soon fell asleep.

"Hey there!" A short male stood leaning over her, shaking her lightly by the shoulder. She looked up, confused, then remembered: she had fallen asleep waiting....

"Oh, I'm sorry, I'm awake now," she mumbled. He removed his hand releasing her and she raised herself to a standing position. "Who are you?" he inquired as she stood facing him. He was a young man: lean, with a dark face and a head too large for his body, which gave him the look of a dwarf.

"Well?" he prompted as she took her time responding.

"I'm looking for Gejza," she said at last. I hope you can help me find him." The man looked at her with an expression of incredulity.

"Did you say Gejza? — Why, and who are you? Are you someone he knows?" he asked warily.

"No, I'm afraid he doesn't." she said apprehensively. "I only know an acquaintance of his; I need some information" — she stopped, uncertain how much to divulge.

"What sort of information?"

"About a friend of his I need to see; do you think you can help me?" she whispered, a note of urgency in her voice.

"I can't help you find Gejza, no!" he said, after a pause.

"Gejza doesn't see anyone — but perhaps I can help you get what you need...?"

She looked at him — hesitating — unable to decide whether he was reliable, whether to trust him, but did she have a choice? Here she is — an uninvited guest — in what appears to be his home: "so far, though strange, he has been treating me not unkindly," she reasoned. "But this may all change once he finds out who I really am. — Should I take the chance and tell this stranger all? It's a risk...it is! On the other hand, he does seem to know Gejza — and it would be such a relief to have someone to trust — to unburden...."

She took the chance. "I'll be brief," she decided. "I'll give the barest details: only what he must know to assist me with a new identity." She began doing that with a sudden burst of resolve and found, to her dismay, that she couldn't stop. She poured her heart out to this stranger holding nothing back and it felt very good to do so.

"Now I'm in your hands," she concluded and stood waiting peacefully, as if determined to take what comes.

"You're more lucky than smart — do you know that?" the man uttered in reproof after a long pause.

"It won't do at all for you to go blabbing to strangers in the way you just did! The rule, as of this moment, is: never tell anything — no names, addresses, personal details — either your own or of people you're in contact with. Give a nickname, if you must, that's all. It's the only way," he continued his instruction. "Take me, for instance: I couldn't help you — or all the others — if people knew my name or where I live. I rent some space here: the people upstairs take my money and ask no questions. I do work for a printer, that's all they or any of the neighbors who might see me here know. You must take to heart what I'm telling you, you hear? Or it'll be of no use to give you documents — understand?"

"Yes, I do! — I promise to be careful. I'm sorry, I don't know why I did that — perhaps I felt I had no choice — I mean, what was I going to tell you? What could I have told you, other than the truth, that you would have believed?"

"You could have said anything — anything at all would have been wiser than the truth, since you didn't know me; didn't know whether I am friend or foe — don't you see? Had I turned out to be the latter, the game would be up for you....It's not just you who is involved here — there is the safety of all of us to think about. Had they caught you looking for us, trying to locate us, the entire operation would be in jeopardy. And we must go on — we must survive not only for our sake but for the sake of the future. We must win this struggle and tell the world all we know. It's a holy struggle this, and you mustn't endanger us!"

The girl was shaken by the depth of conviction and feeling with which he spoke. She moved closer, touched his hand with one of hers and said:

"I swear to you — I swear by everything dear to me — that I will never willingly betray the work you do. I've had my lesson. You can trust me."

"Well, you began with luck, let's hope it will hold," he said, then advised her to follow him across the foyer into the lounge. Here he began by offering her nourishment: a roll with jam and a glass of milk. When she was through eating, he bade her lay down to rest. He took her to the sofa, arranged the pillow and blanket he brought out of a cupboard and advised,

"You should try to sleep a bit now — when you are rested, we'll take care of some of the things you need." She thanked him humbly and a few minutes later was fast asleep.

She never did meet Gejza...nor did she need to: all she needed was taken care of by the benevolent imp, her new benefactor. She had her documents: a new identification card with a name she had invented; the only authentic detail on it being the town of her origin. But it looked very genuine — down to the last detail: the new stamp the Gestapo currently required — and she carried it with her wherever she went. She had some other fake back-up documents in a drawer somewhere — but all of it was better not put to the test. That much she knew. Nevertheless, she walked with assurance these days, her I.D. safely in her pocket, her increasing poise the result of successful evasion — success in having for some time now concealed her true identity.

She works as a maid: assisting in the household chores of a middle aged couple — the Kovačs. The master of the house is a retired school inspector. He is a short obese man with a round very red face and short gray hair. Mr. Kovač walks with some difficulty owing to his weight, but he loves to eat and mealtime is his great joy in life. His attitude toward the girl — who goes by the name of Betka now — is one of indifference. Now and then he gives her a vague smile in passing, most often he would simply walk by her without acknowledgment, which suits her very well.

Mrs. Kovač, the lady of the house, is rather younger than her husband. She is a blond whose short hair is obviously dyed and crimped into tight curls that ring her head. She has an elongated face and watery blue eyes. Her upper teeth protrude considerably giving her the aspect of a horse when she smiles. She is not unfriendly to the girl whom she utilizes also as a companion, but is ill at ease in her role as lady of the house. For, as the girl soon finds out, she had been the maid — or housekeeper as she preferred to put it — before she married the master. She talks constantly, holding back little even of the more intimate details of her marriage. The girl cannot afford to reciprocate: she discloses little of the personal details of her life and has to be constantly on her guard.

The apartment the Kovačs occupy is spacious: one flight up of a fairly tall building in a central region of the city, it is light, with many windows that open outward into the street or yard. It is adequately if not luxuriously furnished: with hangings on the walls and rugs covering the parquet floors. Mrs. Kovač is careful to keep it clean. The kitchen where the lady and her young assistant spend much of their time is large, white and well equipped with the latest in gadgets. The girl likes her work in the kitchen — if only Mrs. Kovač whose name is Irma, wouldn't talk all the time and would allow some relaxation of the high level of anxiety she is under.

One day, as they were preparing one of the countless meals with an eye to pleasing the Master, Mrs. Kovač asked unexpectedly:
"Betka, do you know the recipe for potato pancakes? I'd love to make them but don't know how."

"Yes, I think so," the girl, taken unawares, rattled off the ingredients for the potato latkes her mother used to make.

"Oh, that's great!" exclaimed Irma. "I can't believe it. Where did you learn how to make those Jewish things?" she asked smiling.

The girl stood speechless for a second but collected herself and, mumbling an excuse, ran to the bathroom.

"What an idiot I am — after all that caution — to fall into such a trap. What if she planned it that way? to trap me? To catch me unawares? Who knows how long she has been suspecting me...? Of course, it could be that she does not — that it is a simple coincidence. I can't tell though and, what's worse, now I won't know...now I'll always wonder whether she suspects!"

She was sitting dejected on a bathroom stool not knowing what to do, what step to take to protect herself. She decided to do nothing for the moment. She composed herself and walked back into the kitchen resuming her place at the side of her mistress. "I'll play dumb," she decided, and applied herself in preparing the very dish that might have given her away...!

"Bet-ka-! Bet-ka?" Irma was calling her — and soon appeared in the door of the tiny room the girl occupied.

"Oh, good, you're dressed — I want you to run down to see if you can get us some bread, we have hardly any left. Here are the new ration-cards" — she handed the girl a little packet — "you won't get any without these."

The girl takes the cards, together with the money her mistress provided and places them into a small bag. She hurriedly straightens the bedspread, puts on her coat and hat and hurries along the narrow hallway and out the front door.

She closes the heavy door behind her and steps out into the street. The bakery is not far away and as she turns the corner she can see the bread line already long, growing longer. She is hungry — hasn't eaten yet — and cold. The weather had changed suddenly with an abrupt fall in the temperature. The prospect of waiting in line — who knows how long — frightens her for another reason as well: It is a bad business to be thus exposed. Yes, she has the documents, her official identity, but is it wise to stand around in lines as she must now do? But how can she avoid it? Running errands is part of her job; to refuse to do so under some pretext would be to call undue attention to herself at a time when they may already be suspecting her...

She looks around furtively and fingers the ID in her pocket. It is there — but how good is it? That last stamp..."a good imitation," the fellow who brought it had told her, but will it work? She raises the collar of her coat to shut out the wind, but also for symbolic protection against the malevolent forces that threaten her. "This may be precisely the way Editka was caught..." she is thinking. Poor Editka! Didn't show up at the meeting for the last two months. The two of them had been meeting with three others: young fellows posing as Aryans who worked around the city, but were members of the underground — perhaps Gejza's group? She doesn't know. They know little about what each is doing, where they live or who they really are. They know each other by code name only: hers is Betka, her friend's, Editka. But Editka didn't show up and they haven't heard from her...only rumors that she has been caught persist.

She is jolted out of her reverie by sudden tension and much chaotic movement and noise. The line is being cut off on all sides by a contingent of SS men in full regalia: their glossy black boots flashing; their clubs and guns swinging. They surround the people standing in line and demand documents. The girl is pushed forward by people behind her. Her heart sinks, then begins to race; her knees tremble so violently that it requires all of her strength to remain standing — to prevent falling, face down, in front of everyone.

"This is it, she thinks, the end of the road for me...the dreaded test — the thing I so desperately feared and worked so hard to avoid — it's here after all." One of them is approaching her now and is asking to see her papers. —

"Is this an evil dream, or does it merely seem so to me?" she sees herself reaching into her pocket, pulling out her ID card and handing it to the SS man facing her.

"Surely he must have noticed my shaking hand" she thinks as he takes the card from her and examines it for what seems like an eternity to her. She expects that any second now there will be his heavy hand on her shoulder pulling her out of the line — to accost her with the dehumanizing treatment reserved for victims like her: for Jews. She watches him extend his arm and braces herself to fend off the attack. But the hand at the end of his extended arm holds her ID card, which he returns without a word and moves on. She takes the card and puts it mechanically into her pocket. She pulls her garment tightly around her to steady herself; to conceal her trembling, which she is unable to control and begins walking slowly toward her building. Gradually her fear diminishes: her step becomes light, she experiences elation and joy. Her heart, her senses, sing a silent prayer.

Years later, recalling the incident, she knows it was an Ode of gratitude to the God who rules over life and death.

It's been several weeks now since the incident in front of the bakery. She goes out less these days — only when absolutely necessary for her to do so: When sent on an errand by the people with whom she lives or on those rare occasions when she must go to meet with her group. She is attentive to every word and nuance her employers express — ever watchful for signs of possible suspicion on their part — and in fact she believes Irma has indicated several times: dropping little hints here and there, that she knows the girl is Jewish. Never directly, no, but in hidden messages. Betka is at a loss; she doesn't know how to deal with the situation. She may be in grave danger. But, it is also possible that the Kovačs might protect her if she came to them openly asking for help — as others have done. Somehow she doesn't feel comfortable with the idea of placing herself at their mercy. No, she will find another way. She decides to bring it up talk it over with her group, at their next meeting.

That meeting takes place the following Sunday. There is much discussion about the general situation: The Germans appear to be losing the war (it is November 1944). The Allies are strengthening their positions everywhere, but nothing is being done to relieve the situation for the Jews. Across the border, deportation is in full swing. In their own state transports to the East have resumed: Jews are no longer protected and even the few in hiding or with Aryan documents are being ferreted out.

After the general discussion individual members bring up issues of concern to them, and this is when Betka lays her problem on the table. They consider it for a while and there is unanimous agreement that she must keep her identity hidden.

"Good!" she tells herself: "the decision is off my shoulders — I won't have to lose sleep over what to do." That much, at least, is decided. Although they all agree that there remains the danger – that she must change her situation and fine a new place. She agrees to begin that process as soon as possible.

They linger a while longer after which they all part to go their separate ways.

Betka is walking slowly toward the street where she lives, when she is overtaken by Laci, one of the young men in their group. He apparently lives or works in her neighborhood — or must pass by there? She doesn't known and doesn't inquire. They walk silently side by side for awhile and she is able to observe him. He looks young, but is probably in his late twenties. He is of medium height, with light brown hair and gray eyes. Neatly dressed (his Sunday best?) clean-shaven and wears his hair slicked towards the back of his head. Not bad looking, thinks Betka, and wonders why he is making so little of an impression. It's because he is overshadowed by the others, she decides: especially Sami, their undeclared leader. Sami is brilliant, able to analyze and interpret the most complex situation at a glance; also great at organizing things and a good speaker.

They turn the corner and suddenly stop, not knowing which way to turn, or whether to start running: coming their way from the opposite direction is a German soldier — probably an officer. They have no time to do anything before he has reached them and stops. He begins talking in rapid German, pointing in the direction they just came from. His dialect is thick, unfamiliar, but the girl believes he is asking for directions. It's best not to get involved she decides and her friend apparently has reached the same conclusion: they reply in unison, as if prearranged, in the local language

"Sorry, we don't understand!" and make a hasty retreat into a side street. The German is annoyed and begins the follow them; they part and go their separate ways, the girl running now toward her building. He can only follow one of us now, she thinks and prays he isn't coming after her. She is running, getting out of breath: she is afraid to look back — doesn't want to appear afraid in case he can see her... She does manage to glance over her shoulder and — sees him: he is not only coming in her direction, but is fast closing the gap between them.

"How terrible," she thinks: "If I go into my house (her building is now in view) he'll know where I live; if I keep on walking past the house, he'll catch up with me..."

She decides to cross the street and does so quickly, her crossing obscured somewhat by a passing bus. She enters the building directly across the street from her own and walks up two flights. At the end of the long corridor in which she finds herself there is a window facing the street. She walks toward it and looks out. The German is nowhere in sight. She knows he was there only moments ago — intent on following her. What happened? Did he give up the hunt? Did she really manage to shake him? Oh, if only she could believe that. If only this were the end of that episode. But she cannot remain here in the open... what if he saw her come here? What if he is setting a trap — waiting for her to come into view? She walks down the two flights of stairs, then knocks on the door to one of the ground floor flats and waits. The occupant opens the door: He is an old man with a short grey beard. His clothes, a pair of dark trousers and grayish sweatshirt , are soiled — covered with oil and grime. He carries a toolbox in one hand and with the other pulls the door behind him.

"I'm coming!" he says, "You've got to give me a few minutes to get my things together. I told your mother it'll take a while!" She realizes it must be the concierge's apartment and he is taking her for the daughter of a tenant. She corrects his mistake and in a few sentences tells him of all that befell her: how she was walking with a friend, was accosted and followed by a German soldier, and managed to disappear in this building.

"Can I stay in your flat for a little while — just to make sure the fellow is gone before I go home? I live across the street -? She is about to say with the Kovačs, but checks herself in time.

The man listens with annoyance: he stands there facing her for a while, as if turning things over in his mind. Finally he turns and reluctantly opens the door to his flat.

"Come in here then," he says and motions her toward what is obviously the parlor. "You can't stay here long you know!" he cautions, grumbling. "I am a working man with problems of my own. I can't be bothered with looking after the whole world. You may sit here for awhile buy you'll have to go as soon as I get back, which will be shortly." That said he picks up his toolbox and disappears behind the door to the corridor.

The girl remains alone. She sits down and begins to think about the import of the old man's manner. It's obvious he isn't the friendly type, but is he malicious? Is he capable of doing her real harm? She dismisses that thought.

"First of all," she reasons, "he doesn't know or suspect who I am. Therefore, he cannot really hurt me. Then, complaining is probably all he does; he seems to be the type. Well a little bit of time here — waiting out of sight — is better than nothing."

It turns out that his work in the tenant's flat takes much longer than he anticipated. By the time he gets back it is dark and safe for the girl to return home and, without much further hesitation, she does.

She relates her experience to Irma, carefully leaving out her meeting with the group, who stands at the door as she enters. Irma is angry:

"Where were you all these hours?" she asks accusingly. The girl tells her, but meets with little empathy.

"You should have just come straight home," Irma scolds. "Go get your supper. It's ice cold by now," she offers. "Then you can wash the dishes and straighten out in the kitchen. I'm going to bed."

Betka does as she is told and retires as soon as she finishes her chores. She can't fall asleep and the later it becomes the more anxious she grows: she worries about her safety here. In addition to Irma's possible suspicion she now has an additional reason— the German — he may have seen her enter here. No, she must go! And if go she must, why not now — before she gets into trouble here? She sits up in bed in the grip of a sudden urgency — hysteria of sorts— to leave immediately.

She gets off her bed and very quietly, with great caution, finds her bag and begins putting her few possessions into it. She is very careful to take nothing that doesn't belong to her, leaving behind even the few personal articles Irma had given her: a comb, a change purse and sweatshirt. She must avoid cause for accusation that she took things that didn't belong to her. She is ready in a few minutes. She looks at the clock: it is two o'clock in the morning. She is afraid to walk around in the middle of the night, but decides that she has no choice.

She is surprised to find that she feels no guilt at leaving here without a word, but the fact is she doesn't. "Am I ungrateful?" she wonders. "After all, they did give me shelter, even thought they didn't realize... well, I must go before they hear me. She makes her way slowly to the entrance hall, opens the front door, is careful to close it quietly without any noise and begins walking toward her destination.

She knows where she is going, for there is only one place she can go to now: to her friend Berta. When Berta had spoken of an emergency, this surely is the type of situation she had in mind? She tries to recall the exact words; what was it Berta had told her then? She remembers...

"Let's make up a signal, so I know it's you when I hear someone knocking in the middle of the night."

"A signal?"

"A certain way to knock on my door. A code, which only you and I know about, so I can be certain it's you."

"I see. O.K., that sounds important — mysterious, too. What shall it be then, our code?

They agreed upon a definite sequence of knocks on the door. The girl stops a minute trying to recollect the signal, succeeds, and resumes her walk, determined. This is the middle of the night and she is in such need. She has only a short while to go from here and it's safe — way too early for anyone to be about. She accelerates her pace and beings to feel excited. It will be good to see Berta after all this time. "God! — All of the turmoil I've been through since we last saw each other! How long has it been now?" she thinks, trying to approximate the length of time since she had left the city. "It was the eve of Yom Kippur... that would have been toward the end of September. We're at the end of December now: it's three months only — hard to believe — it seems more like three years... but it will be good to rest, go nowhere, stay somewhere close to Berta for a bit."

She arrives in front of the building and looks around. The street is still quiet, not yet awake to the approaching day. She listens but can distinguish none of the sounds of an awakening city. A deep silence reigns, broken only by the forlorn barking of a distant dog. She feels alone.

She walks through the open door and up the flight of stairs. She stops on the landing in front of the door to the workshop. She gets into position, extends her hand, knocks in the agreed upon manner: three short knocks following each other closely, two knocks, then a pause, then one knock. This she repeats three times, and waits. Nothing happens. She repeats the entire sequence once more, and waits again, then after a while, one more time. There is no response...

She is dumbfounded. Had Berta forgotten about the whole business? She considers that possibility, but rejects it. No, Berta would not forget a commitment like that. There must be another explanation: Berta hadn't heard her. She either isn't there, or is asleep. Knowing Berta to be a light sleeper, she dismisses that possibility as well. No! Berta either isn't there, or wouldn't open for some reason. "Well, what difference does it make?" the girl thinks. "Why Berta didn't open the door? The fact is, she didn't. I'll have to accept that. No good standing around here knocking: I don't want to call attention either to Berta's presence here or to myself. I'll have to disappear from here as fast as possible. But what to do? Where do I go from here?

She stands a while thinking and suddenly, out of the depth of her memory, a name flashes through her mind. "Rozsika! Of course, Rozsika will help me! Why didn't I think of her? I know she will help!"

She relaxes then, for she will not have to go. Rozsika works in the bakery downstairs. All she will have to do is find a place to sit down and wait quietly, out of sight, until the bakery opens.

She comes down the stairs and instead of going through the front entrance out into the street, she finds the door leading into the back yard and goes through it. She silently slides by the door to the back entrance of the bakery, whence come the sounds of workers finishing their nightly shift, and enters what looks like a storage area. Here she stops a while to look around, she opens the door to a closet, closes the door after herself and sits down on the floor to wait.

"I'm glad you came to me! Don't worry, we'll do something, we will have to, won't we?" Rozsika whispers and winks at the pale, exhausted girl who barely manages to stand upright.

"I know you must be frightened and exhausted, but after you eat something it won't be so bad," she says, hustling the girl into the back room. "Remember this room and our meetings with Berta here? Berta, h-m, you say she didn't come to open the door? I wonder what's going on? — I haven't seen her for the last few days. I'll have to look into that — but first, you! Let me see... I have an idea!" She rushes out of the door, motioning to the girl that she won't be long.

When she returns a few minutes later, her plan has been set in motion. It now remains for her to inform her young listener of its details.

"Here is what we will do," Rozsika tells her. "You will probably be able to stay with Miss Šulekova. She is a seamstress and needs someone to help her. A very fine woman: a spinster, she lives alone. I told her I have known you for a long time and she wants to give you a chance. She is willing to train you in return for your help and give you room and board. The best part is that I think we can trust her: we may be safe in telling her the truth — that would be so much better for you, don't you agree? — but I want to think about that. We must be certain! In the meantime you'll come home with me. You can stay in my house while I work — my father, who lives with me, won't mind. He is a friendly old man. We will think about it for a few days and then decide."

The girl is relieved and grateful. She makes herself useful in the back room. Toward the evening, when Rozsika closes up shop, she takes the girl home with her.

CHAPTER FOURTEEN
THE SEAMSTRESS

Rozsika lived on the third floor of a walk-up flat in a low-income part of town. She had notified her father that she is bringing the girl home with her and when they arrived they found him waiting in the kitchen. He was an amiable old man: short, with a sparse amount of thin grey hair and a toothless grin. He was engaged in preparing the table — in the corner of the kitchen underneath a large window — for their evening meal.

Rozsika unloaded the parcels she brought: fresh bread, a cake and a bag of groceries she had purchased that morning. Some of them she placed on the table where they will be immediately needed, the rest she handed to her father who stored each item in its appropriate place.

The girl stood by the window watching the woman and her father interacting as they laid out the meal. The old man, she could see, enjoyed the trust of his daughter who appeared to rely on him for much of the work while she was away. She addressed him fondly, yet not without a measure of condescension that rose to the surface now and then. Nevertheless, he responded with affection and pride. Indeed, he very likely indulged every one of his daughter's whims.

The old man's compliance, his eagerness to help — Betka would soon realize — served some of his own needs as well as his daughter's. He was a man used to work, with no apparent leisure habits. He didn't read, for instance, not even the newspaper, relying on the street corner — where he and his cronies gathered — for news and gossip. He no longer worked away from home and so spent most of his time and energy keeping the apartment tidy and functioning.

They ate their supper hurriedly: a light meal consisting of vegetable soup, bread and some compote made of apples and prunes, after which the girl retired for the night. Rozsika had suggested that Betka remain at home during the day when she, herself, was at the bakery: "It's safer that way..." she said. They all agreed and the girl prepared herself for the task of assisting the old man in his household chores.

The next day went by fast. She familiarized herself with the small apartment and offered to do some of the work while the old man went on his errands. True to her resolve, she completed the chores he would otherwise have to do, well before he returned, then sat down at her assigned corner of the kitchen table to leaf through an old magazine she found on a shelf. There was not much privacy for her in this apartment: no separate room to retreat to. Rozsika's single bedroom held a double bed, which she now shared with the young girl; the old man slept on a cot in the living room, apparently his permanent lodging. It was quiet and restful sitting here alone, but her attention wandered from the pictures, advertising and short superficial descriptions of the home furnishings the magazine catered to. She peered out of the large window into the street, but only from where she was sitting — she didn't dare approach the window, didn't want to be seen.

She was thinking, as she anticipated the return of the old man, of the best way to keep herself occupied without intruding upon his activity and space. She wanted to be of assistance, yes, and was quite comfortable as she did the chores while he was away. But the need to be here with him for any length of time caused her discomfort and unease. It was such a small place — they were bound to be at each other's heels wherever they turned. He seemed friendly enough and was probably well intentioned, but she felt not a shred of the kinship for him that she had for his daughter. Indeed, the mere need to communicate with him made her uncomfortable. And he will soon be back...she didn't relish the thought.

She was relieved, therefore, to find Rozsika unexpectedly at his side when he returned shortly after the noon hour.

"I decided to look in on you quickly — so, how is it going? Did you do all this by yourself?" Rozsika feigned disbelief as she walked around examining the tidy apartment.

"Well, well, I may yet reconsider this entire idea of sending you to live with someone else," she laughed. "Speaking of which, I haven't had the chance to talk to your future employer yet: we were very busy today, but I did reflect about the matter, and got further confirmation about her character. Judging by what her acquaintances say, she is a 'trustworthy woman who wouldn't harm a fly.' Of course, the acquaintances don't know about our problem, but I have the feeling she is humane: disapproving of the things that are going on. I think you will be safe to disclose your identity to her. This is my opinion, but you understand that the decision must come from you? I can't make it for you."

"Of course, I understand. Thanks for your advice though — I shall heed it. God, it will be a relief to be able to speak the truth...not have the threat of discovery and betrayal hanging over my head!"

"Good! I made an appointment with her. We shall go over there as soon as she calls — in a few days, she said. Until then you will have a rest here with us."

"How lucky I am to have a friend like you!" the girl mumbled rushing over to embrace Rozsika who held her for a while then walked her to the table where the old man had already prepared some lunch for them all. They ate and talked until it was time for Rozsika to return to work.

"I'll be home before you know it," she called to the girl before she went out the door.

"I know, don't worry, I'll be fine. — "

Betka returned to the kitchen. The old man was putting away the leftovers and the girl helped him carry the food and dishes. She assisted him in washing and tidying up, then excused herself and went to rest on her part of the bed, having secured his permission to do so. She closed the door eagerly, anticipating a bit of solitude — wishing to think through the path she must soon embark upon. Alas, she didn't think for long, she soon fell asleep and by the time she woke Rozsika had returned.

The next day began well. In the morning after her friend departed, the girl helped with the chores while the old man went on his rounds. She reminded him to bring the shelf paper, for they wished to surprise Rozsika. The shelves in the kitchen cupboards needed relining and the old man was willing to help her do it while his daughter was away.

He came home early, as promised, and they began the task. They worked for a long time and Betka thought they will never see the end of it. She was discouraged by the mess around them when all of the contents of the cupboards — pots and pans, glasses, china, flatware, groceries, and countless other utensils that go into equipping a kitchen were everywhere on the floor. But finally they managed to do it all. When they closed the last cupboard holding the freshly washed sparkling earthenware, the girl felt great satisfaction along with her sense of relief. She was able to give something to Rozsika, no matter how little. She was about to retreat to seek a bit of privacy when the old man said to her:

"Why don't you come to the table, Betka? I think we deserve a treat now — having worked so hard — don't you agree? We can have some cookies with milk, what do you say?"

"Good," the girl replied. She hadn't felt hunger all the time they had been working, but now, thinking about it, the prospect seemed appealing. She made her way to the table and slid into a seat opposite him.

He brought the milk out of the icebox and placed a small plate with sugar-topped cookies in the center of the table.

"There, have some! These are not from the bakery, you know? My daughter makes these herself. They are quite good."

"Thank you, I will have one." They ate their snack in silence. When the girl saw that the old man finished eating she rose from her seat.

"Shall I take these things away now?" she offered, pointing to the milk and leftover cookies on the table.

"No need to hurry, I might have some more in a little while. Why don't you come a bit closer though, to my side of the table, so we can talk. I'm a bit hard of hearing, did you know that? Yes, I will have to get one of those things some people have — he pointed to his ears — to make them hear better, you know? — It might help a bit! Well...? If you're not moving, I shall," he proclaimed; he got up and moved to a chair next to the girl's.

He appeared to hesitate, then, "You might even consider giving the old man a hug, no?" he said and brought his head so close to hers that she could feel his breath in her nostrils. She became frightened by his sudden move and repelled by the unpleasant odor emanating from his mouth. She rushed from the table, ran to her bed in the next room, slammed the door behind her and made sure the latch was fastened. She didn't move from her bed until she could hear Rozsika talking to her father in the kitchen two hours later.

She had been pondering her dilemma all this time. Should she tell her friend about the incident? Or is it better to remain silent? It all depended, she reasoned, on how long she must remain here.

"Perhaps the old man had no evil designs and I overreacted" she pondered. "But it was so sudden...so unexpected, and he frightened me so!" Oh, he makes it so unpleasant for me to remain here now; what will I do? It won't be the same! I feel harassed and afraid...well, I must wait and see!"

Rozsika called her and she got off the bed. "I must conceal any trace of anxiety for the moment," she decided. She carefully combed through her tangled curls and made her way to the bathroom where she washed and dried her face. Only then did she emerge to greet her friend. The latter had already discovered the freshly lined cupboards and embraced the girl thanking her.

"What a wonderful surprise," she told her. "I'm really sorry to let you go: now that you've proven yourself so wonderful," she added with her usual mirth, but it's all arranged. You'll come with me tomorrow when I leave, and she'll pick you up at the bakery. See that you have all your things together. We'll have to leave here early.

Betka stood in silence, taking in the information. "Thank God!" went through her mind. "I never thought I'll be eager to leave here...how sad, but what a relief! I won't have to mention anything — I can put all of that behind me." She hurried into the bedroom, put all of her things into the old bag and retired for the night.

Miss Šulekova was very tall: a woman in her late thirties probably, with long yellow hair that was artificially curled and a fair, somewhat faded, complexion. She was rather thin, which magnified her height and gave her a slouching appearance. Her eyes, of a watery blue color, were set high in her face, which was dominated by a prominent nose. The nose was the feature Betka became aware of at once: not only was it large, but it was hooked as well — definitely a Jewish nose. (Betka and her friends in the underground had become sensitive to noses: it was one way they were able to pinpoint one another). If she hadn't known better, she would have suspected Šulekova...but no, she was assured by Rozsika that it was not the case. "I'll have to be careful," she warned herself. "If they should detain us on account of her appearance, I will be the one to be caught...I must be seen with her as little as possible!"

Her new protectress lived in an old house, up on a hill, off the main road leading to it. There were several apartments in the building, hers facing the front — the street entrance. You came into a long narrow hallway. The first door to the left was Šulekova's. She opened the door. They entered a large rectangular room: gloomy, the ceiling high, almost out of sight. A bit of light came in through the small window in the wall to the left of the entrance. This was the kitchen, holding a stove, cabinets against the far wall, an icebox and a sink with a water faucet coming out of the wall. Facing them (from the entrance) was a door that led to a fairly large square room. Here there was a large window and the walls were white — making the room light and airy. There was a large table piled with fabrics, pattern books, several kinds of scissors, sewing baskets with threads, needles, buttons, ribbons and other equipment needed in the trade. By the window that looked out to the street was a large sewing machine with a chair next to it. The door on the far wall (opposite the one they came in through) led to Šulekova's bedroom and a small washroom. This was it.

"Where will I sleep?" wondered the girl — "in the kitchen? On a cot in the sewing room?" But she soon found out. Next to the cabinets in the kitchen (in the corner on the side of the entrance wall) there was a door. Behind it was a tiny (long but very narrow) room with a cot and a nightstand. There was no window here — the space was very likely intended for a closet — so it was quite dark; the light bulb hanging from the ceiling had to be kept on day and night. This became Betka's room — her little private domain. Here she could retreat to think and to cry, whenever she needed to be alone.

Šulekova was not unkind: she showed the girl where everything was kept and told her what her chores will be: she will have to assist both in keeping the house tidy and in preparing the clothes to be made. Unless there was some urgent work, she reserved the mornings for household chores and shopping. The afternoons were for sewing (extending often into late evening) when

175

clients were likely to appear bringing their projects or trying on their unfinished garments. She taught Betka to do the "finishing," a task the girl had been familiar with from her experience in a neighbor's workshop.

On weekends there often was company. Šulekova had a friend who would come to visit and stay till Monday morning. He was a man in his fifties, probably, but vigorous and fit. A hunter, he dressed for the role: tall boots over britches tucked into them, a short double-breasted jacket and a Tyrol hat with a feather in its band. His demeanor was somber: the girl never saw him smile. He brought venison when he came, on which they would feast during his stay. Occasionally he accompanied Šulekova into town — to see a picture show, to walk, or meet with friends in the local tavern. Betka would sit at home and brood.

Brood? Wasn't she satisfied? Wasn't she happy? Wasn't this she had hoped so fervently for only a short while ago? — to have a place where she was safe without having to conceal the most important part about herself? Yes, and yet…there was a sense of frustration and restlessness. She didn't know why — couldn't quite put her finger on the reason. Perhaps because of her relative safety here…because she didn't constantly have to be on her guard — the normal expectations of a young girl, so long repressed, began to find their way to the surface. She, too, desired action, experience — yes, even fun. But here she was, sitting alone in her room shut away from all that was going on in the world around her.

She didn't know, had no clue whether their weekend visitor knew her true identity. Šulekova had introduced her to him only as "Betka, my new assistant" and had mumbled his name at the time, but the girl hadn't made it out and never did find out his surname. She subsequently herd Šulekova call him Peter and he remained Peter in her own mind. But Betka and Peter largely avoided each other, while taking each other's presence for granted. She never asked her patroness whether the man knew. She largely avoided reference to him. Šulekova, on the other hand,
 did talk to her about her friend: that he is a successful business-man living on the outskirts of the city; a kind-hearted and honor-able man taking care of his mother and that she had known him for many years. She seemed to take pride in his friendship. Al-though the man wasn't given to affectionate display, he appeared to share her feelings.

It is a Tuesday morning in February. The snow outside covers everything for miles around. The trees nearby are white specters, their branches heavy, weighed down with snow. The windowpanes are covered with frost. The wind, strong all night and into the early morning, is showing signs of slackening somewhat. Betka has just risen. She washes and hurries about the kitchen to prepare what is needed at the table for breakfast. They are expecting a client who is bringing material for a new frock.

The morning meal is sparse: bread with a bit of cheese and coffee. After the table is cleared and the dishes washed, she joins Šulekova in the workroom: they open the shutters, resuscitate the slowly burning fire and sit down to wait. Soon the figure of a young girl — wrapped in a woolen scarf over a heavy winter coat — appears on the winding path that leads to the house. She walks up slowly and stops before the door to catch her breath. She then approaches and rings the bell. Šulekova admits and welcomes her smiling:

"You're braving the weather! It's a bit windy out there isn't it? I wasn't sure you'd come today."

"I know! but I have to go to work anyway and I haven't much time left. I told you I need this garment next week. Will that be agreeable?"

"Yes — I will try! I cannot promise that I'll have it for certain. There is always something that may come up to hinder completion. All I can promise is to try. When did you say the wedding is going to be?"

"Next Saturday. I do hope you can manage; here is the fabric. What do you think?" The young lady, who had managed to remove her outer garments by this time, brought out a blue satin material intended for a gown from a little pouch, together with some lace, ribbons and a lighter fabric for lining. Šulekova examined it carefully then nodded in approval.

"Yes, I think this will do very nicely for what you have in mind. Here, why don't you sit here by the fire and look at these books!" She handed her young client several pattern books and showed her to a chair by the fireplace.

"There are several items here you might like. Take your time — I'll join you in a little while."

"Thank you," said the young woman politely. She took the books, walked to the fireplace and sat down where she had been shown.

Betka, in the meantime, busied herself with the finishing touches — a hem in this instance — on a skirt that was to be picked up that evening. But every now and then she would glance with hidden admiration at the young woman in the seat by the fireplace, for she it was, or rather her behavior, that Šulekova held up to Betka as a standard for emulation.

The young girl was much surprised the first time her benefactress had done so. "Why?" she wondered, "what's wrong with my behavior?" She felt peculiar, her pride wounded at being rated not quite on a par with Elenka (the young woman). Yet, she was forced to admit as she observed the latter, that there was something in her bearing if not her looks that set her apart. Yes, there was a quality about her manner — a quiet poise that betrayed confidence and self-esteem, which she, Betka, was certainly lacking. She was forced to admit it, much as she disliked to do it. In addition to her poise, Elenka was good humored with a special kind of sweetness. Indeed, it was easy to pinpoint the contrast between the two of them, Betka being sensitive, self conscious and often ill at ease. "But who is she (meaning Šulekova) to tell me that? She is not my mother! And it isn't fair to compare people like that — and our circumstances so different! After all, don't I have some good points she doesn't?" Still, Elena did become something of a model to her — someone to emulate, even though she wouldn't admit it consciously.

Afterwards she often wondered why — why did Šulekova do it? Why did she criticize and lecture her? She seemed to take such pleasure in it, too.

"Listen to Elena...pay attention to the well-mannered way she speaks and behaves; she has such charm, such poise...." The words cut her like a knife. She feared she could never approach Elena's charm rooted in a personality as different from her own as day was from night. Yet Šulekova implied that she only needed to emulate Elena for these delightful attributes to become her own.

The obvious answer (to her many why's) which Betka didn't realize at the time was that Šulekova saw herself in "loco parentis" vis-a-vis the girl. She did what a mother, or other responsible adult in charge of guiding development, might do. The girl, however, wasn't in a position to appreciate her efforts, she resented them. Even in retrospect, her mentor's criticism of her manners, of her behavior, seemed unjust to her: too eagerly given, somewhat cutting in tone, so that whatever benefit the criticism might have brought was thereby lost. Is it possible that this was a way on the part of the seamstress to ease the frustration and anger she felt? Not at the girl, no — she was too refined for that. She did enter into the agreement to protect the girl voluntarily, after all. And yet, she may have felt helpless, trapped in a situation that was by no means easy for her — one she didn't really want to be in. Criticizing the girl's manners in the name of "bringing her up" was perhaps a way to went her anger without being overtly destructive. But Betka didn't understand the complexity of the situation. She was hurt and resentful.

They are sewing away one late afternoon when the sirens begin to screech. There have been daily air raids lately, some with disastrous results. Usually Betka remains in the apartment, fearing exposure to neighbors more than the danger from above. This time, however, Šulekova insists that she come to the shelter. She complies.

The so-called shelter is a large unfinished room in the basement of the house. Crude makeshift benches have been installed around the walls. On one side of the room there are a few shelves holding some dishes and foodstuff and an old kitchen stove. There is also a table and chairs in one corner, presumably for dining, should the necessity arise.

The room is dark as they enter from above and Betka cannot make out the others present. As her eyes adjust to the dark, she recognizes Mrs. Hruba, the obese matron who lives in the apartment above them and her old mother Mrs. Erna. It is in the middle of the day and the men are not yet home from work: "I do hope this one doesn't last long — and that it will not do us much harm — the old lady remarks in a high-pitched tremulous voice as she takes her place near her daughter.

"Hush, mother, all we can do is wait!" responds her daughter, cutting her short. She is used to lord it over her parent, a widow, who has been living with her for some years. "If rumors are correct, we can expect to sit here till midnight and who knows

179

what we shall find when we venture out of here. Her statement is cut short by muffled sounds, not unlike that of rolling thunder, that seem far of, but soon become closer, louder and last for quite a while.

"My God, this sounds too close for comfort," says Mrs. Kovalska, a trim woman of about forty who usually wears a cheerful expression. She now moves her hands upward as if to cover her face. It is a sudden involuntary motion in response to her fear.

"It's those blasted Jews and their protectors. It's on account of them that we sit here and suffer," opines Mrs. Hruba after a prolonged period of silence. She appears to have swallowed the propaganda of the radical faction , which she now regurgitates intact. No one contradicts her and she turns toward Betka who is standing nearby and has suddenly turned pale.

"Don't fret, my dear. Sit down next to me — here, she moves over and points to the vacant place beside her.

"Thank you," mumbles the girl in a barely audible voice. She walks over but sits down next to Šulekova who is aware of her distress and moves to make room for her. They sit and wait, spending the rest of the time in speculation and in gossip. At last, after what seems an eternity, the signal calling off the raid is sounded and each party returns home.

"It's the last time I have gone down," says Betka when they have returned home, "Why so? — at least we know that she doesn't suspect. Don't you think it's valuable to find that out?"

"Perhaps, but I can't take it — I cannot stand by and listen to that without being able to utter a word in defense. — No, I don't want to be present...."

"I understand!" Šulekova wisely changes the subject.

They find out the extent of the damage that very evening. One of the industrial sections of the city suffered direct hits. Buildings were destroyed, some of them residential and there are numerous casualties. The fires are still raging...Events such as these disrupt their lives periodically, but the girl and her benefactress, like others around them, slowly resume their usual routines.

Betka, though now less exposed to the danger of sudden betrayal than she was before, has nevertheless retained contact with the boys from the underground. She has been attending their regular meetings and learned important bits of information concerning events in general and particularly what people in her position needed to know.

One day, Latzi informs her that a certain Mr. Fuchs is making inquiries about her. Not by name of course, he doesn't know the name, but the description he gives of the person he is looking for fits her!

"Inquiries about me? But I don't know anyone by that name — why? What does he want?"

"To know where you are, to find you."

"Don't you dare tell him! No, I don't want anyone to know where I am! Someone is suspecting me...wants to betray me!"

"Don't worry, we can't tell him what we ourselves don't know! No one knows your address — it's part of our policy — remember? But I'll make inquiries. If I can find out what's behind it, I'll tell you. We can then decide what to do."

Betka returns home somewhat reassured, but still uneasy, unable to free herself of the fear occasioned by knowing that someone is on her trail.

At their next meeting it all became clear. The grandfather, having heard (through the underground grapevine, though it puzzled the young girl how they came to know who she was. As far as she knew, the only time she had revealed her identity was that first night in town to her friend the "imp".) that his granddaughter lives somewhere in town, left no stone unturned to locate her and have her join him in the bunker. So, the personage known to everyone as Mr. Fuchs, one of several "miracle men" who kept those in hiding informed and supplied with much of what they needed, was set to the task of locating and bringing her over. No one else could have done it. but Mr. Fuchs was known to the boys in the underground as trustworthy, and so they agreed to cooperate with him.

So it was that at one of the meetings Mr. Fuchs presented himself to the girl and handed her a note. The girl opened it and saw at once that it is from the grandfather. In it he pleaded with her to come at once — to join him without much delay.

The girl stood before a dilemma: Should she go? Should she return to her grandparent who obviously wanted her to share his life now — but was it wise? Should she change course at a time when things are relatively safe for her? Along with her safety here,

181

she had acquired a measure of independence. She had taken crucial steps in her life all by herself, alone. That hasn't been easy: she had often felt the bitterness of solitude, of isolation, of having no one to consult or to rely on. Especially in times of transition, when friends she came to know and need were suddenly gone — no longer there for her. No wonder she was so easily overwhelmed by gratitude towards the few friends she now had....But being on her own had also been a liberating experience. She liked some of the things she had learned to do for herself. Is she to give all that up now in exchange for a life of dependence? Of becoming a child again who needs to be protected?

In the end her sense of filial responsibility — aided in some measure by prompting from Šulekova, who perceived an honorable way out of her own responsibility — won the day and the girl agreed to go. So it came to pass that one cloudy morning she said her final goodbye to her benefactress. They stood on the stoop in the front of the house; Šulekova, still in her morning robe, her thin blond hair loose, embraced her. Betka was surprised to see a tear appear on her cheek as she bent down to hug her.

"Good luck...take care!" she whispered. "I know you'll be fine!"

"Yes, thank you — thanks for everything..." the girl turned to face Mr. Fuchs standing near his car a few paces below them. "This is it..." she mumbled following him into the vehicle, and they were on their way.

CHAPTER FIFTEEN
THE BUNKER

The place to which the emissary, Mr. Fuchs, took the young girl was an isolated hut that stood in the middle of an orchard in the hills of the city. The orchard was part of the grounds surrounding a rather large house inhabited by a childless couple, Mr. and Mrs. Škoda. The man was a railroad official who was rarely at home. His wife ran the household assisted by her boarder (lover?) Janko: a tall gaunt young man, recuperating from a recent illness.

Janko, a Jew, had taken the initiative of transforming the hut in the orchard — that must have once accommodated the cooking needs of a large household — into what he now called the bunker. The structure had two rooms: the front room, the kitchen, was narrow but long. It was dark, without any windows, and had to be artificially lit, but was well furnished with the necessary, if outmoded, equipment and gadgetry needed for preparing large meals. (The Škodas no longer used it for that purpose: they had a newer kitchen as part of the house.) Adjoining the kitchen was a small rectangular room that had two small windows high up on the wall opposite the door. This room may have been intended as the cook's bedroom. Now, however, it had a long table in the center with chairs all around it. There was nothing else here.

The girl arrived towards the evening hours of a weekday. Mr. Fuchs ushered her in, stayed awhile exchanging small talk with the inhabitants and departed. The girl waited until the grandfather, having just finished his mincha prayer, came out of the inner room to welcome her. He embraced her and held her awhile, then released her saying:

"You came just in time for the Megilah, you know?"

"In time for what? She couldn't believe she heard correctly — Me-gi-lah? why ..."

She was given no time to be perplexed. She followed the grandfather into the little room where all stood assembled. On the table, which was covered with a white cloth, was an open scroll. One of the men stood bent over it, preparing to read the story of Esther, the Purim story, to those present. The girl stood in wonder, as if recalling a long vanished dream.

"Purim? Queen Esther? Megilah? Yes ... it was all coming back now, but from far, far away...from a time long gone — surrounded by misty fog. So, they are reading the Megilah here as if nothing had changed and she — why, she was hardly ever aware when the Sabbath had arrived or departed...."

They must have noticed her disbelief, for one of the girls approached her saying:

"I know how you feel. It seemed incredible to me too. but I'm used to it now. We do it all quietly of course, in an undertone, you see?

No, she didn't see! she didn't understand, but accommodated herself quickly to their routine as she had to do wherever she was and to their assumption that what they did was safe. The Škodas did have watchdogs and any outside movement was met by a barrage of barking. There would be enough time to clear things away, cover the traces and disappear, if anyone came....

Disappear? where to? She wondered about that and tried to imagine a likely hiding place — but why bother? She will soon find out.

After the reading of the Megilah, there was a festive meal prepared in advance to which everyone, except the grandfather and Rabbi Heller, another eminent personage with them, contributed their labor. The girl liked the way the men shared in preparation, serving of and cleaning up after the meal. It was all arranged in the beginning: no one able to work was to be exempted from the daily chores. The men did the heavier work: the lifting of pots, buckets and cauldrons, but also shared in the regular chores. Cooking, baking, cleaning and laundering — they took their place along the women in all that had to be done.

Toward the end of their stay, there were sixteen of them in this shelter: ten men and six women, not counting Janko, the proprietor, who stayed in the house with the Škodas. He would join them on a regular basis, whenever there was any matter to be decided; anything that needed his counsel. He was part of the enterprise, but came to share the quarters only when needed.

The bunker began with a few regular inhabitants, cousins of Janko, then the numbers gradually increased, as each brought in someone too precious to leave behind. Among the first were the three brothers Loeb, cousins of Janko. One of them, the eldest, brought in his fiancée, Rela, who brought along her sister Lola. Then came the Loeb's cousins, another couple of brothers bearing the family name. There was a young couple, the Fabers, also related to the Loebs, whose infant was in shelter with another family in town. Rabbi Heller and the Stolers — father and son — joined them after escaping from a train bound for Auschwitz. The grandfather, as the girl knew, had been allowed to join them early on, and he later brought her, his granddaughter. She, toward the very end, brought her friend Berta, whom she was able to contact through the intercession of Mr. Fuchs.

She is relieved at the change of scene: It pleases her to be among others with whom she can share her fears and the small pleasures the place afforded. She throws herself with zest into her assigned place. The rest of her first day is spent observing the people around her, getting to memorize their names and listening to their stories. The man who more than anyone draws her attention is Rabbi Heller. He is a burly individual with a large round face covered with brown stubble (all that remains of his thick bushy beard that had to be cut). He is a brilliant man— a nationally recognized leader of the community who, prior to his capture and deportation, had been involved in major rescue work. (His efforts, in collaboration with other leaders, held at bay deportation in this state for almost two years. He and the other members of the committee known as "The working Group" had been instrumental also in attempts to save the Jews in the neighboring state. They had access to the top ranks within the German command, but lacked the money that was needed. Success in their efforts to obtain the funds as well as cooperation for their schemes from the Jewish leadership in unoccupied Europe, in Israel, and in the United states, was elusive, at best.)

Rabbi Heller managed to jump the train on the way to Auschwitz, but couldn't forgive himself for having done so. The girl would see him pace the room (whenever his attention wasn't diverted by some pressing problem), wailing loudly, accusing himself of a litany of crimes:

185

"Who am I that I should survive, while they [his wife and children and all the other Jews on that train and on all the others] went to their death? What good am I now, dear God!? by what right am I here? Why should my presence here endanger the others? — for I have no right to live! It was my responsibility to save them — and I failed so miserably! How can I ask forgiveness — when I cannot forgive myself? What did I fail to do? What should I have done?" The stream of self-abuse went on and on, accompanied by anguish and suffering — by a lament that could have come only from his soul.

The young girl found these manifestations of his guilt disturbing at first, but soon learned to ignore them — as did everyone else. They all accord the Rabbi sympathy and respect, but go about their tasks without comment. It is the only way to function.

Mr. Stoler, and his young son Roni, are another matter. They, too, had successfully evaded extermination — returning, as they did, from the "threshold" of the gas chamber. They too must have their regrets at abandoning their loved ones — but bear their pain in silence. They are a cheerful and courteous pair: the older man providing encouragement and dignity, the young boy enthusiasm and cheer to their group endeavors.

The Loeb brothers and their cousins are a pragmatic lot, dedicated to the proposition of solving problems and making things work. They spend little time in theorizing and less in brooding about things past. Their diligence and cooperation in getting big and little tasks accomplished, is what makes life in the place bearable.

The two young women, Rela and her sister Lola, are important assets to the "workforce" in the place. Both are young and lovely to look at. The older one (Rela) has beautiful features: light brown hair, large hazel eyes, and high cheekbones. She is slender, with a lovely figure and a winning smile that reveals beautiful white teeth. Her younger sister is shorter, with less striking features, but with a lively disposition. She is a brunette with a head of curly hair and mirth that often ends in ringing
laughter. Much of the cheer in the place comes from her ebullience and willingness to be of help.

Then there is the young couple: Livia, a pretty young woman with blond hair and her husband, Tibor, a bit older, of strong build and dark complexion. They are very much in love, cannot help being demonstrative, though they make an effort at restraint. It is the first time the young girl is able to observe the signals of young married love at close quarters. There is a makeshift swing hanging in the doorway of the vestibule leading into the kitchen and the two of them spend time around it whenever they have a few moments. They flirt, chase each other, and engage in other forms of affectionate play when they find themselves alone. Everyone is sympathetic to the young pair who had to rid themselves of their new baby girl before entering the bunker. (They placed her with a non-Jewish friend of Livia's, the wife of the local police chief, as it happened. They know she is safe, and are relieved at being so fortunate.)

It is late in the evening of that first day, the day Betka arrived here. There had been much to do: She met the people, listened to their stories, memorized their names and assumed the chores assigned to her. The meal she had helped prepare has now been eaten, the dishes washed and put away and the rooms tidied. The men are now in the dining room reciting the evening prayer; The women are gathered around Livi, who is relating a funny incident from her school years. Soon it will be time to go to sleep.

This is the moment the girl has been waiting for. There had been no mention, so far, of where they will sleep, nor has she been given any clue of where that might be. But now the time has come: They are in the dining room seated around the table. After a while, one of the young men rises: he pushes aside the chairs near one end of the table and bends towards the floor. He removes part of the rug, then gathers up his strength and slowly, but firmly lifts up two of the floorboards: he removes them and places them side by side against the wall. He then removes another two and does the same. There is now revealed a rectangular hole in the floor about three feet wide and five feet long. One by one, the occupants — gathered around the opening — make their way onto the narrow ladder that stands in the hollowed out space underneath the floor. The elders and the women are being assisted down. When all are inside, Janko, who is here for the task, replaces the boards and pulls the rug back into its place.

Care has been taken to remove any traces from the rooms that might indicate uses other than the preparation of food for the family in the house up front. The rooms are now bare, dark and silent and remain that way all night.

In the bunker, coming down the ladder, one descends into a narrow longish space. In the far corner of one wall a small electric bulb throws dim light over the area. Looking around, the girl sees that the entire space to the right of the opening is filled in by wooden shelves. Each of the shelves is divided into compartments and each of those houses one or two occupants for the night. The space assigned to her is in the cubicle occupied by the two girls: Rela and Lola. The two of them squeeze together to make room for her, the newest occupant in the bunker.

Some have sleeping bags, others spread out blankets to soften the impact of the hard wood on their bones. Only whispering is allowed here, and soon even the dim night-light will be out, leaving them in total darkness. Rela, anticipating that, points to the area to the left of the entrance where a large chamber pot stands on the ground.

"It's for an emergency only," she whispers to their young friend. "We try to use it sparingly."

"Of course, I understand," the girl replies. "It isn't pleasant to go with everyone present." Nevertheless, there is some activity around the pot every night: the older people are unable to wait much of the time, and quite frequently the younger ones too must use it. The first time she had to do this, in the middle of the night, Betka found it very hard to make her way in the dark. She had to be careful to step over, not on, the sleeping people around her, then do the same thing on the way back. She had been instructed to carefully replace the lid, to minimize the odor... and did so. In the morning the pot is emptied and washed, the bags and blankets stored and the bunker, prepared for another night, is left empty while the occupants move around in the rooms above, going about their daily chores.

Occasionally this routine is upset, as on the day when they heard sudden barking and unexplained movement in the orchard around the hut. They immediately left everything they were doing and scuttled into their hiding place. Within moments everyone was below ground. Mrs. Škoda came in unobtrusively: she replaced the boards and hid other evidence of their occupancy. They listened to her movements with bated breath, noted when she left and remained where they were for the rest of that day. That evening they heard from Janko who let himself into the bunker in a prearranged manner, and told them of a group of soldiers camping nearby some of whom had strayed into the orchard ...

It's all clear for now," he added and handed them some rations of bread and cheese (brought, among other provisions, by their good friend Mr. Farady: a former business partner of the Loebs who, not being Jewish, lived in the city, and made it his chief business to provide them with food. He did this on regular visits to the bunker, often spending considerable time bringing them up on important news of the day.) and water. The next day they were able to resume their usual routine.

Although they tried very hard to cooperate with each other in carrying out their collective needs, they could not avoid occasional grumbling by one or another of the occupants (mainly among the younger ones), nor even open conflict now and then. There were simply too many of them here: their space too small for total amiability. The matters over which they fought were trivial, the quarrels conducted in whispers and stopped abruptly upon the entry or attention of a significant elder.

It is April, 1945. They are all lined up by the entrance to their hut each holding a bundle of their most important possessions. They are waiting for the conveyance that will take them to the place where the trucks are waiting. They are embarking upon a risky journey: they will travel in German army vehicles accompanied by SS personnel. The deal was arranged by one Reszö Kastner, a Jew with access to both the German high command and the American Jewish community. The Germans are to get one thousand dollars for each Jew they bring out from German-occupied territory and deposit at the Swiss border.

The question they (the occupants of the bunker) have been pondering for some time was: should they go on this journey, at the mercy of the Nazis every moment of the way, or should they stay where they are? Each alternative holds grave risks: if they remain in hiding they may yet be caught and sent away in the last minute. They also fear the impending occupation by Russian troops. The news wasn't good for women, especially. On the other hand, if they went, who knows what will happen to them? After much discussion most of them (with the exception of the young couple who had their baby in town) decide to go, wishing to avoid the chaos of the Russian liberators whose entry was imminent. So here they are, waiting to be taken to the German cars..

PART V

SPRING 1945:

DEPARTURE

CHAPTER SIXTEEN
THE JOURNEY

Two large transport trucks stood waiting for them when they arrived. There were just the fourteen of them at first, the young couple (Livia and her husband having remained behind. They eventually found shelter with some friends in a nearby village). And Janko — "I have no desire to go" he informed them and remained where he was, in the big house, assisting his landlady with her daily chores.

The front of the vehicle in which they find themselves is occupied by the driver and two others: — very important personages who sometimes ride together up front and at other times take turns accompanying the refugees — it is they who made these transports (another one started out from a different direction) possible. One of the men is a German officer with the rank of Obersharfuhrer; the other is Kastner, the privileged Jew with influence who had arranged the deal with high-ranking Germans on their behalf. He is permitted to come and go freely, isn't required to wear the yellow star, the special sign of the Jews, and acts in the capacity of consultant to the Germans.

Kastner is a heavyset man of medium height. Of light complexion, he has a round protruding belly and the rest of his body is well fleshed out. Judging from his looks, he must be a man in his forties. He makes much conversation with the German officer and at times also engages Rabbi Heller, who sits not far behind him in the compartment they all share — the back of the truck.

The German, who answers to the name of Nazdaleny, has been in a position of authority for some time. He had been in charge of matters concerning the Jews in the state — especially the transports — and is known to be "a man you could work with" — one, in other words, who might be induced to take a bribe, providing it was lucrative enough. Now he is anxious to secure as much as possible for himself and disappear.

Officially the money the Germans get in this exchange (an exchange arranged through the mediation of Kastner between the Germans and the Swiss) is supposed to secure trucks for the army, of which there is a grave shortage now. It is rumored that for each Jew brought out of the German occupied territory and deposited in Switzerland, they are to get a thousand dollars. The money is to come from America — mainly from the Jewish community there. They (the refugees) are content to know as little as they are told about the matter. They ask no questions. They ride in German army trucks, under constant surveillance by (and apparently with permission of) the SS high command. They are at the total mercy of the Germans and they don't know — as they fall sleep each night — whether they will see another day.

They embarked on this venture in the middle of Passover and took a few packages of matza. Yes, they baked matza in their kitchen. For an entire week they did practically nothing else and they took what was left with them. This is all they eat now and must carefully ration and divide up the small allotment for each day.

Their journey is taking them through Austria and Germany, all of it territory under siege. Since they ride in German army vehicles, they are especially vulnerable: several times the trucks are forced to make unscheduled stops — the last time in a forest — and the refugees are told to get out. They huddle under trees during an attack by Allied planes, trying to avoid the bombs aimed at the German trucks. (At a designated point in Austria a group of people — brought here from the concentration camp at Terezin — has joined them. Two other trucks were put into service and they now form a convoy). They ride by day and rest (when they can) by the road at night. They travel in this fashion for a long time, their progress being constantly interrupted: either by air raids or by personal matters attended to by their German escort. They sit and wait thus often (sometimes for days), wondering whether they will ever reach their destination.

But it is only a matter of time: within a few days from their last derailment they resume the road and soon reach their long awaited destination: the Swiss border. Here they are met by the Swiss border guard (an intimidating lot) and ushered into a waiting room: they will have to undergo lengthy medical examination, a cleansing procedure, after which they will be placed in quarantine for several weeks. Only after all of this will they be allowed to join others in a special home reserved for war refugees.

They witness in silent awe the brief transaction between their German escort and the Swiss border police. A joint sigh or relief involuntarily escapes their throats when it is over: acknowledgement that they are here at last — out of the German orbit, in a free land — among the lucky few who succeeded in getting out of that tortured hell of fear. Yes, they are free at last! They made it!

CHAPTER SEVENTEEN
FREEDOM

It takes a few days for the realization that they are really free, to sink in: That they no longer have to fear discovery that they are in no danger of being caught and sent to Poland. However, the routine here in the compound they share with other refugees from different lands, all of whom are undergoing the "cure", reinforces their sense of restriction: for the Swiss who treat them and supervise their action are very strict: the refugees must submit to a schedule designed to rid them of whatever infection or infestation they may be suffering from. They must all undergo the routine — even those who are free of any visible problems.

Eventually it sinks in: they are here only temporarily. They will soon be able to move around freely among other free people without fear of being detained on account of their birth as Jews. So they submit to the routines: they apply the ointments, take the medication, do the required exercises with zest for they know it will soon be over: they will be left alone in the end each to pursue their private goals. In the meantime they are together, doing what is required of them and spending the few private moments in the attempt to locate their loved ones.

The young girl spends much of her time with her friends from the bunker. Together they explore their immediate surroundings and revel in the beauty of the snow-covered peaks in the distance. The panorama of the mountains from here is breathtaking: every morning the spectacle seems different. Though the mountains are the same, the play of sunlight, mist and color upon them and the way all this is reflected through the mirror of the vast lake deep down in the valley, results in incredible changes in view. They stand around speechless, stunned by the beauty around them, drinking it in eagerly.

The girl also likes to observe the adults around her, among them her friend Berta: the last one to have joined the group in the bunker. Berta, like the rest of them, had decided to come along on this journey. She thinks her chances (once out of quarantine) to locate her fiancé are better from here, where she will have freedom of movement for her inquiry. In the meantime the girl follows her around and is fascinated by some of the details of personal hygiene Berta now has time to attend to. She teaches her young friend how to care for her hair, how to nourish her skin, especially the face, and helps her develop a routine of exercise, including walks around the premises.

Finally their task here is ended and they are taken to Lausanne, a nearby city. They are settled temporarily in a hotel with other refugees, until their more permanent location is decided upon. They are refugees, and as such are not permitted to join the Swiss citizenry in many of their civic privileges. For instance, they will not be able to work here. Only citizens can do so. Nor will they be able to obtain citizenship (their grandparents must have been citizens). But temporary stay is being granted them with provision for their maintenance, part of the cost for it being supplied by the Swiss government.

In the hotel they meet a number of individuals (mostly middle aged people) from Germany and Austria and the young girl is introduced for the first time to the way in which they chant or sing the Grace after Meals. She is fascinated by this custom — thinks it is attractive and tries to learn the tunes.

Here their routine for them is somewhat relaxed. Their lodging and food are supplied by the hotel staff. There is a set schedule for the meals, which take place in the dining room; their rooms are supplied with bedding and linen as well as other necessities, but, unlike in regular hotels, they must do the cleaning themselves. Their time is their own. At eleven P.M. The outer doors close and they must all be in. This is for reasons of security, but until then they are free to use their time as they please. Their shelter here is temporary — until a more permanent refugee home, now under conversion, is ready.

At last they are in a very beautiful spot: in a lovely village in the "Berner Oberland" above Lake Thun, or Thuner See, as the Swiss call it. They came here on a special train designed for climbing mountains. A fairly large hotel, converted into a refugee shelter, is their home now.

They were welcomed, upon arrival, by their director: a bureaucrat by the name of Funk. Mr. Funk has his office on the premises and is there most of the time. He is in charge of all their affairs: the intermediary between them and the Swiss authorities, he supervises all that goes on in the home.

They arrived and found some residents (refugees from other areas of Europe) already there. They have their rooms, which are Spartan, but clean. The girl and the grandfather are in separate, adjoining rooms. The kitchen is staffed by refugees like themselves; (they are not allowed to be gainfully employed, but that doesn't mean that they are not expected to work). Many take their place in work units running the home. Mr. Funk is in charge of these assignments. This work appears to be voluntary, since not all of them do it.

The first time they are ushered into the dining room Mr. Funk appears and makes a formal speech. He welcomes them in the name of the Swiss people and invites them to take part in a meal prepared for the occasion. The main course on the menu today (as it is to be most days, they later discover), consists of "Sardinen mit Pelkartoffel" (sardines with potatoes cooked in their peals). The potatoes are freshly cooked and the sardines are large and taste delicious. (It is only after months of unvaried consumption that the girl feels she never wants to look at another sardine mixed with potato). They greatly enjoy this first meal however.

After the repast Mr. Funk proceeds to lay down the law. There are certain rules, he informs them, designed to assure the smooth orderly running of the home, which is his responsibility. He expects order, civility and strict adherence to regulations.

Mr. Funk is very tall, well over six feet. His blond head is elongated and his mien is serious, even dour. His voice is deep. The effect is intimidating. While friendly, he is reserved and maintains distance: he isn't easily accessible for a chat; should one need him, however, he can be reached.

The girl soon becomes involved in keeping house for the grandfather. Basic food is being provided by the hotel kitchen. However, the grandfather requires special dishes both on account of his diet (he has diabetes) and to provide desserts for the people who come to seek his counsel. This requires a routine of some shopping, cooking and baking, not to mention cleaning the rooms on a regular basis and she finds herself occupied most of the time. In the late afternoons, though, and on many an evening, she finds time to cultivate her old friendships and to seek new ones. She finds several girls her own age whom she is eager to befriend, and also women — both young and old — for whom she develops regard and affection. This is a period of joy for them all: they are able to resume their interrupted lives.

The refugee home resounds with the bustle of activity that characterizes normal life: life without fear. Most of them are now engaged in the serious attempt to locate their dear ones (liberated from the camps or from hiding) and the lucky ones: those who obtain the good news, soon leave, to become reunited with members of their family who are alive. The grandfather sends out messages everywhere: perhaps Uncle Simon (whom people had seen alive in the various camps until well into 1944), perhaps some of the others (her parents, her siblings, her numerous uncles, aunts, cousins), but the news isn't good. There is no trace of anyone — not a single individual of their large family seems to be alive. Not one of them has made it out of the camps.

The same fate appears to have befallen most other families in the home. Among those in the bunker most lost all their loved ones. The exceptions were the two young girls: Rela and Lola, the sisters, whose mother had been in hiding and remained alive and the Stolers, father and son, who regained one member of their family: a young boy, liberated from the camps. Berta, too, after much effort, heard of her sister's whereabouts: her sister was alive and was to rejoin her soon. But not the person she most desired to be reunited with: her beloved fiancé. No! He didn't come back! Berta spared no effort searching...a task that occupied most of her waking hours. She wrote letters...often from early in the morning until late into the night...she stood in interminable lines, appealed to all agencies looking into these matters...she left no stone unturned, but without result: there was no trace of her fiancé — he did not return!

To say that she was heartbroken would be to gravely understate the matter: she could neither eat nor sleep for long periods of time. She prayed, reciting portions of the Psalms whenever she had a spare moment; she wept, pleaded and implored the Almighty for mercy: to grant her the happiness union with her betrothed one would bring her. She walked around red-eyed, with her prayer book in her hands, like a shadow: distraught, full of grief, to begin the same cycle again on the morrow...

The girl was now in her upper teens. For her upcoming birthday the grandfather surprised her with a lovely pair of diamond earrings (obtained with the help of Mr. Stoler who knew stones). He chose for her a pair of small studs (about 35 points each) that glittered remarkably because of their beautiful, unusual color. "They are blue-white and flawless, that is why it doesn't matter if they are small," he explained. No, indeed! it didn't matter that they were small. That's what made them acceptable to the girl who was embarrassed to wear diamonds. She put them away for special occasions. But She cherished them as a token of the grandfather's love for her, which he manifested in many ways.

Although she was very young, elders around her now began talking of a suitable marriage partner for her. There were several young men in the home who showed interest. One of them sent his aunt to inquire whether she might accept his advances. She thought about it...had seen him walking in the company of a fellow student to and from the yeshiva study hall located at the far end of the grounds.

The young man lived in the home with his father and his aunt and uncle, the only other members of his family. He was a tall, lanky youth with ginger hair and complexion. One of several students of the newly created resident yeshiva (led by Rabbi Seif, a well-known scholar and resident of the home who had come here with another transport brought out of German-held territory by the man who had organized theirs), he was bright: did well in his study and was intellectually inclined. But he didn't appeal to the girl. No, she couldn't see herself married to him. (Nor to anyone else for that matter.) His aunt, speaking on his behalf, told her later (after she had rejected the idea of his advances) that he was heartbroken.

"He can't eat and won't get out of bed. He is so sad, nothing will console him! — are you sure you won't see him? He really is in love with you...!"

The girl was astonished. She tried to imagine, to visualize the young man lying in his bed, his thin frame covering the entire length of it; his long legs stretched out, the large feet hanging over the bed. She could hear him reject food and clothing, the way his aunt had described it, and refusing to get out of bed. She wanted to bring forth empathy with his suffering for which she was apparently the cause, but found herself unable to do so. The vision she conjured up elicited mirth, rather than sorrow. His emotional state left her indifferent, if not cold. Yes, she was sorry (in an abstract sort of way) about his suffering, but couldn't enter into or share his emotions. She thought the matter strange and soon dismissed it from her mind.

There were other would be contenders for her hand, providing mirth for her and her friends. Berta, especially, would tease her about this, but also instructed her as to the limits of her choice:

"He will have to be someone the Rebbe (the grandfather) approves," she insisted.

"I know! but he can be someone we both favor — can't he?"

"Yes, of course!" Berta reassured.

Time was passing fast now. She was occupied most of the day with the household, but found some diversion in the late afternoon and evenings, walking about and talking with her friends. Sometimes she walked alone. Their refugee home stood in the midst of a group of hotels (it had formerly been a hotel) on the outskirts of the village, catering to the tourist trade. They were high up in the Alps and all sorts of people came here for holiday. They were mostly young skiers and she loved the spectacle of watching them rush down the nearby slopes. Every day, between the hours of eleven or so in the morning until about three in the afternoon the sun would come out in full strength (even though it was the middle of winter; as long as there was no blizzard) and everything began to glitter in its radiance. The air became quite warm, like in the summer and the skiers could be seen removing their outer garments and rushing down the slopes with their arms bare. The glitter of the sun was beautiful on the snow and ice spread all around them and its warmth in the midst of this winter wonderland added to the sense of exhilaration.

Some of the skiers were soldiers on leave, among them Englishmen and Americans. It was the first time the girl saw uniformed men belonging to the Allied forces. (It might have been some of these, she reflected, who were in the planes throwing bombs on the German trucks they were riding in: the time they had been forced to vacate the vehicles and hide in the forest until the raid was over. Who knows?) It was also the first time she had the chance to observe people engaged in this sport: it seemed to be great fun, exhilarating even to watch, and she stood silently by enjoying the spectacle. She could participate only vicariously in this activity: this part of life here in the mountains was remote — out of reach to the refugees. They hadn't the means, the time or the inclination for it. And even if the rest of them had somehow managed to become part of the sport, it would almost certainly be barred to her, like everything else that was fun ...

After all, had she been allowed to join the people in her own group — the other members of her bunker — on their recent excursion to the Jungfrau? Of course not! Everyone had gone except her and Berta. Berta, too, had judged it inappropriate to don slacks and join a group composed of men and women who went to seek merriment amid the peaks in the Alps. The grandfather had declined to give permission for her to go: it is unseemly, he declared:

"You must keep in mind that you are different. You cannot participate in an excursion with men on board. No, this is not for you! not for us...!

"Right! not for me. Whenever there is a bit of fun to be had, count me out — it's unseemly!" she mused with longing and a bit of resentment. "What am I to do?"

She caught herself thinking about her isolation quite often, wondering about her future — about the things it held for her. She wasn't ready for her future; certainly not for marriage. There were so many things she didn't understand, didn't know the answers to, that she would have liked to know, to learn. She understood that the world outside (beckoning with its seeming attractions) would provide satisfaction to her curiosity and might gratify the core of her emotional need. She sometimes longed to break out of her shell to become part of that world, but knew that she couldn't — at least not for the present — and she drove these thoughts out of her conscious mind.

What to do? Employment was out of the question: she wasn't fit for anything, had no skills and her status as refugee would prevent it even if she had. Another more crucial reason was the grandfather: he needed her: she was all he had — all that remained of his entire family, and he clung to her; couldn't bear to let her out of his sight. Moreover, his need to cherish her was not oppressive. He was loving, generous, and courtly in his conduct toward her. She felt she had a wonderful parent: a source of love and hope that many of the people around her lacked. She was grateful, if not entirely happy with her lot. Nevertheless at times her longings and doubts would surface suddenly:

"Shouldn't I be thinking about extending my education — about going to school? I have missed out on so much of it during the war!"

Education, unlike active employment, was a real option. It was an opportunity the Swiss did not prohibit. Even refugees in their midst were allowed access to some of their schools, and many took advantage of it precisely because it was a dignified substitute for work. The knowledge and skills one acquired could then be utilized to work elsewhere. Several young people in the home went off to school. But she could not. Schools away from home were not an option for her. She must remain where she is: at the side of the grandfather. It was not only that he expected no less of her; she had come to expect that of herself.

There was one skill she was able to pursue right there in the home, however. One day she read an announcement describing a sewing workshop soon to be offered those who wished to acquire that skill. It sounded interesting: it was to be taught on the premises, by a professional seamstress (one of the refugees) who lived in the home. The workshop was offered by ORT, an organization created in Europe at the turn of the century designed to provide Jewish youth in transition with much needed skills, to provide them with some type of livelihood. This was a project she could pursue. She applied to be admitted and soon became one of its most diligent artisans. She learned not only to sew, but to cut the pattern according to measure and she took great pleasure in creating a garment.

205

She made a dress for her friend Berta, her first, and was a bit nervous when the time to try it on arrived. How proud she was when, during the trial, she realized that it was a perfect fit:

"I can't believe this, you don't need to alter a single pin; not a stitch needs to be changed!" exclaimed Berta, very pleased, and the girl was proud. She made many another garment, both for herself and her friends, and later carried the book of instructions, written in German, to the States with her, along with the excellent little portable sewing machine the Swiss were producing (Elna), that could be opened up and operated on top of a table. (She bought it second hand, for a trifle, and only after arriving in the States, where it sold at exorbitant prices, did she realize the bargain she had.)\

She now had a skill in hand: some possibility for employment if she ever needed it, as well as a means to keep boredom away in her present situation. She found contentment in her craft: the process of creating something out of nothing, as it were, never failed to amaze her. (She had admired that ever since her early school days, when sewing instruction for at least two hours each week had been part of the elementary curriculum. It had not been her strongest suit. One day, in exasperation over the sloppy appearance of her work, her teacher had exclaimed: "Anča, I am afraid we will never make a seamstress out of you!" But she had loved the activity even then and later, in a neighbor's workshop, though she had only meager opportunity to advance her skill, her admiration over what could be done had grown.) She took great pride in her ability now and it provided satisfaction — a sense of triumph: she could do it after all!

They were leaving the home! It had been a decent temporary shelter for them and the other people it housed. Slowly people began to leave, seeking to reestablish themselves permanently — to make a new life where they could remain. For the grandfather and herself there were several options: the land of Israel (then Palestine), the United States of America, or somewhere in Europe. The first step however was to transfer themselves to the city, to an urban environment, from where the task of emigration could be more fruitfully pursued. Thus it had come about that one sunny morning the young girl, the grandfather and most of the members of the bunker arrived in the Swiss city of Zurich. Here they dispersed, each into their own place, which had been previously arranged for, but still in proximity to one another.

She and the grandfather settled in a small apartment in the Koch Strasse, in a section of the city inhabited by middle class elements: merchants, artisans (some professionals and students) a number of them Jews. The grandfather had sponsors here: the family Kessler, who helped find the apartment and accommodated them in their own house when they first arrived. The Kesslers were Swiss citizens: they were born in the land and their parents who had been immigrants had managed to become citizens themselves. The family had three children, the youngest born just recently when the young girl and the grandfather were already in residence here. The Kesslers occupied a large flat: the upper story of a duplex they owned jointly with another branch of their family (the sister of Mrs. Kessler, her husband and children). The aging parents of the Kesslers lived in Zurich as well and so did numerous people who, like the Kesslers, had made it their business to show hospitality to the refugees, especially the grandfather and his young charge.

Thus it was that they found themselves quite comfortably ensconced in their own flat, which was sparsely furnished but clean, if not yet cozy. There was a bright kitchen painted white, two small bedrooms and a large living/dining area part of which served as the grandfather's study and reception room. The girl could now run the household from their own private flat, though they were hardly ever alone. The members of the bunker who lived here in town became frequent visitors and there were others: acquaintances and strangers alike coming to visit; to pay homage to the grandfather. These people had to be welcomed and the young girl soon found herself with a full time job on her hands: she was responsible for the provision of all that was needed in the household and though she had some help with the chores, the task of supervision became hers. The grandfather, though unable to render physical assistance, provided guidance and emotional support so that the task, even when exhausting, was manageable.

The grandfather was now assuming his proper role — the functions he had been engaged in before the war. True, he had no pulpit here: he wasn't serving as a communal, nor even as a congregational rabbi, but his role of Hasidic leader — the Rebbe whom people sought out in order to receive counsel and a blessing — he was able to and did assume. He was one of the two Hasidic leaders of pre-war stature (Hasidic leaders who had established followings before the war) presently in Switzerland. The fact that he survived the war and the circumstances under which he did so became known to the remnants of the Jewish community — the survivors — and people began to flock to the small residence on Koch Strasse. Not having a regular pulpit meant that he had no exact income: no designated yearly sum paid by either a party or an institution. But income there was, nonetheless: for, according to custom, those who sought him out to pour out their hearts and receive his blessing invariably brought material gifts, most often in the form of funds. Thus it was that the grandfather and his household became increasingly well provided for.

The matter of resettlement now began to assume some urgency. The Swiss had made it clear from the start that their assistance was to be temporary: their country serving as way station for the refugees on the way to a permanent home. Of the different options for resettlement the grandfather considered (Palestine, the United States, or elsewhere in Europe), the most appealing place to go to seemed Jerusalem, the traditional haven for aging Jews. One wanted to be buried in the Holy Land anyway: since they must seek a new home, it might as well be their Holy Land. Thus it was that they went to Geneva. The Consulate and officials they needed were here and they spent the better part of six weeks in the house of the family Gross — people from their own region who had been living here for some years:

The Grosses were not recent refugees; like the Jewish-Swiss families in Zurich they were permanently settled in the land. They were a family with many children of all ages, not especially well-heeled: they struggled to make ends meet, but found room for stragglers in their city and were now accommodating the grandfather and his entourage: the young girl and two of the Loeb cousins who were here to assist with the leg work. There was much work to be done: bureaucratic red tape had to be cut at every stage in order to even get on first base. When they finally got there they found that nothing could be done to get them into Palestine legally: The British would not permit it and they sadly returned home without the Affidavit, the document that would gain them legal entry necessary to fulfill their dream.

Europe was not a real alternative for the grandfather. Back home there was nothing: empty communities, devoid of Jews or any semblance of Jewish life and nothing could be revived here. Western Europe may have been an option, but they had no sponsors with active interest in their coming there, and so they settled for the United States. It was a time when Europe lay in shambles, needing decades to recover from the war whereas America was full of vitality and of great possibilities. There were people in New York, old friends — adherents of the grandfather and his family — willing to pave the way for their coming and so it was that they undertook the initial steps in the lengthy process of emigration to America.

The young girl and the grandfather went to the capital city of the state they had lived in before the war, for a lengthy stay. They needed papers in preparation for their journey to America and this had to be seen to. As on their trip to Geneva, they brought along a couple of the young men from the bunker to help with the bureaucratic difficulties and to accompany them on their trip east. While there they sought to retrieve some of their personal possessions.

Thus it was that one fine spring day, in 1946, the young girl found herself in her hometown. It was a strange experience. Everything looked the same, nothing seemed changed: the streets, the houses, the shops — they all looked as she remembered them. Only the people, her people, that is, were no longer there. They were all gone. She walked around the streets in disbelief; she felt like being in a ghost town, or a graveyard. And nobody seemed to miss them. There were people everywhere walking, shopping, going about their daily chores; nobody stopped to comment or think about what had transpired here such a short while ago.

At one intersection she ran into an old woman whom she had seen working in some of the Jewish households here:

"You are here?" she asked the girl in astonishment, "I thought you were dead!" the girl, shocked at this crude reception, mumbled something and quickly made her escape. She did find a young Jewish couple, one of the beautiful daughters of her neighbors (the sister of Rudy) who returned from the Partisans together with her sweetheart. They married and now had a small infant.

Life did begin anew, even here, but they were the only two people in town and they did not intend to stay. They came to retrieve some of their property and will soon make their way abroad.

She was glad to have seen them, but decided to look after her own business that brought her here: retrieval of some property she and her mother had given for safekeeping to one of the business people in town, the local miller. She arrived during a somewhat inauspicious time: the day of the wedding of Mr. Szoltes' daughter, a girl only a year or two older than herself. They were all busy with the wedding. Mr. Szoltes, looking festive in a new black suit and gleaming white shirt came out to meet her. He seemed preoccupied, but recognized her and acknowledged the receipt of her family's property. Unfortunately, all of the linen and clothing they had brought him was later confiscated by the Russians, he claimed.

"Only the silver is here. I can return that to you. Come back tomorrow, and I will give it to you."

She thanked him and departed. Her plan to look up some of her non-Jewish classmates who had been her friends, or some of her teachers she had adored, she now pushed out of her mind. No, she will depart here as soon as possible; she couldn't bear the indifference: it was as though these dear people had never existed. Nobody cared!

The next day, true to his word, Mr. Szoltes handed her a large box. In it she found the four silver candlesticks that had been her mother's to light the Sabbath candles in and her father's large silver menorah for Chanukah. She looked at these items for a few moments then took the box. She thanked the man for preserving what he could for her and made her way to the car waiting outside to take her back to the grandfather. She was done here!

Their next stop here in the eastern part of the state was to the town her great grandfather had lived in. Here they found a number of Jewish families who had returned. They stayed with one of these for a short while, as long as necessary to retrieve the few cartons of books that remained in the library of her great grandfather. Yes, the books were all here — only the people to whom they belonged were missing. They took what they were able to and, in the morning, their business at the capital done, they returned to Switzerland.

She brought a lovely set of crystal (a cake service for eight) as a gift to the Kesslers and mementos for her other friends as well. She also brought a number of items for their household as well as clothing and footwear for herself and the grandfather. All this was in preparation for the journey — their journey to America. It will take a few months before all of the necessary documents will be available and that time could be utilized to prepare themselves, to assemble and pack the items they wished to take along.

Their friends were helping with these tasks. It will be hard to say goodbye to them, to their Swiss friends, the people who had shown them so much hospitality and kindness, and, of course, to their friends from the bunker. That will be hardest of all. They had spent a long time with each other: they seemed like members of one family by now. But there comes a time when even members of the same family must separate — say goodbye to each other — and that time was soon upon them. The girl was sad as she went about her chores these days. Yes, there was excitement in anticipation: she will soon be embarking upon a new life, in a new land...but her future was so uncertain, her goals so unsettled. What will become of her? In the short run she will take charge of the grandfather's housekeeping — she knew she will have to begin with that. But what then? Well, she will see...

The day finally arrived. She stood there, in the street in front of their flat, surrounded by her friends who came to see them off. (The grandfather didn't want to fly. That meant they will have to go by boat. The steamer selected for them that will take them across the Atlantic was the SS Nordam, a beautifully constructed Dutch tourist-class ship. The journey was to last eight days and they were to leave from the Dutch port of Rotterdam. The plan was for them to stop in Amsterdam with the
family Rubin, remote cousins, and travel to Rotterdam a day before the ship was to depart.) The plans were all set: the luggage had been sent ahead, only a small valise with a few personal necessities for each of them was standing in the street with them.

The girl felt forlorn, unhappy. She looked around the small group of assembled people and wished suddenly that she didn't have to go. She regretted to leave behind, part with, several of the individuals she had grown so very fond of during the last few months they had spent together here.

"My God, another one of those wrenching leave-takings," she reflected. When will it ever stop?" She felt bereaved: she wanted to be comforted, loved, cherished. Someone should be here to hold her, wipe away the tears, take away the hurt, hold out some hope! Her friends did embrace her exchanging parting endearments, but it sounded hollow and she felt no comfort. Somehow they didn't feel her pain, or so it seemed to her.

It was time to go. She took a final look back and stepped into the waiting car. The grandfather was already in the back seat in the company of Nathan (his newly arrived nephew, a young man in his late twenties who had come back from the camps and has been making his home with them). She joined the driver in the front of the car and they took off to catch the train.

CHAPTER EIGHTEEN
A NEW LIFE

They embarked on Friday afternoon, about an hour before sundown. The boat was to leave the port on Saturday morning. It was December 7th, 1946. They were to travel for seven or eight days and arrive in New York around December 15th or 16th. The grandfather shared a room with Nathan. The girl shared quarters with two other women: the wife and daughter of a Dutch diplomat residing in New York, returning from a vacation in Europe.

The daughter was a young woman of about twenty-five, very pretty: tall and slender, with blond hair and blue eyes. An experienced traveler, she appeared accessible and willing to instruct the young girl about the ways of the world. They communicated in German, for the girl knew only a few English words; her fellow lodgers, the mother and daughter, spoke English to each other.

"I have traveled on this beautiful ship before. Do you want me to give you a tour of its many different areas?" Ingrid, (the daughter) inquired.

"Thank you, that will be nice!" the girl replied and they set out.

"Good! Let me show you the dining room first" Ingrid volunteered taking the younger girl by her arm. They went up the stairs leading to the deck and several large spacious rooms adjoining it. One of these was the large, spacious dining area. There was one substantial oval table seating about twelve:

"This is the Captain's table." Ingrid informed her. A beautiful bouquet of fresh flowers stood in a shining brass bucket in the middle of the table. The gleaming damask tablecloth hung loose on all sides. The chairs around it were made of highly polished oak, matching the walls in this room, which were oak from floor to ceiling. There were about a score of smaller tables in the room surrounded by similar chairs.

"This is where we eat," Ingrid pointed out. The seats are assigned in advance. A fortunate few eat at the Captain's table, the rest of us wherever we are assigned. But you will see for yourself tonight."

"No, I won't. Grandfather and I will eat together with Nathan in their room. We must have special kosher food, you see? It was all arranged in advance. Most of it will have to come out of tins, I think, for they have no kosher kitchen here."

"Oh, that's such a pity! The meals are so delicious and such fun! The entire process, I mean. It's a shame you'll have to miss that."

"I know! But I'm used to it."

"Well, don't worry. You'll have plenty of opportunity to see the Captain in action. He also talks to us occasionally and then there is the dancing and music in the evenings. Here, have a look at the ballroom — it's where the parties and dances take place. Also the cinema. Look, it's on now!"

The girl joined her friend in one of the many chairs around a large screen. The vast room was empty and dark. On the white screen an animated cartoon of Mickey Mouse was in progress. The girl was fascinated: She had been to the cinema before the war: had seen movies imported from America about a charming little girl with a head full of curls whose name was Shirley, or "shirleika," as the young girl and her friends called her. They each collected picture-cards of the beautiful little actress and would trade with each other. But this was different. She had never seen one of those and she liked it.

They sat here until the end, then rose to continue their tour.

"You should see this room when there is a dance! It is bright and lovely here and the sound of music from the live band is wonderful. I'll have to introduce you to some of my friends — you'll need a dancing partner, you know?"

"Oh, I don't dance! I mean I have never been to a dance before and I wouldn't know what to do."

"You'll learn very fast, I'm sure. It isn't hard, you just follow the man, you see? They have to lead, but come here, I'll show you. She grabbed the girl and led her to the dance floor where she swirled her, in step to the rhythm of the Blue Danube strains, which she herself supplied. She was a good leader and the girl found it easy and irresistible to dance along with her.

"You see? It's easy isn't it? I told you!"

"Yes, it is, her young companion laughed, agreeing. And it's fun. But I probably won't be able to come, you know.

"Why ever not?" Oh, there will be plenty of people here who will dance with you, don't worry!"

"No, it isn't that, the girl replied, it's just — " She left it at that — why explain? They decided to continue their tour later that day and the girl went to visit her grandfather.

She didn't continue the tour of the ship that day, nor, indeed, the day after nor the day after that. She was ill: she couldn't walk, nor even stand; her head was turning, she was feeble and very nauseated. She wasn't able to swallow any food without bringing it back up again: she vomited everything she had eaten since they arrived here, it seemed. The best thing for her was to just lie on her bunk, face down, so that is how her fellow lodgers found her day after day. The strange thing was that neither Ingrid nor her mother was ill: they were seasoned travelers, it seemed, and hadn't succumbed to the paralyzing state that afflicted her.

Ingrid came close to the bed, as she had done a dozen times before since the girl fell ill:

"Anny, you cannot continue like that! You must get hold of yourself, dear." she admonished. The girl knew she was right, but couldn't do anything: she tried to raise her head, but the room began spinning as soon as she did so.

"I can't — I did try, did you see I tried to raise my head? I'll just have to wait...oh, this misery, when will it stop?" She let her head fall back again and just lay there: her eyes closed, her hands limp by her side.

"I'm going now," Ingrid said, "but I'll be back in about an hour. "Then you will have to take something. I simply won't let you waste away here. I think you will be all right, but you must be willing to try!

"O.K., I'll try, I promise!

Maybe that was it, she reflected. You must be deliberate and gain the upper hand. She will try...but now she must rest. Yes, what a relief just to rest, oblivious to everything...

The grandfather and Nathan were also ill — both of them apparently as inert as she herself. As soon as she had that information, she made the effort to get well herself and she soon did. It lasted only two days for her, whereas they were ill for the better part of the journey.

The meals, when they could eat, took place in the grandfather's quarters. Dinner was served them at the same time as the rest of their shipmates. But their food came out of cans that had been brought on board. Nevertheless, it was appetizing: on special new trays and dishes and nicely garnished. The meat or fish were always warm and served with fresh potatoes and vegetables (boiled for them in special pots), and fruits. The girl ate heartily: she had eaten nothing during her illness and her body craved nourishment. Yet the memory and sense of her illness (the nausea), lurked in her consciousness — close to the surface. It seemed that at any moment a thought, a feeling, or odor would tip the scales and she would be ill again. She worked hard at such moments to retain equilibrium — and remained in control.

Now came an exciting time for her: she was in proximity to the grandfather, could visit when she wanted to, but had a bit of freedom as well. It was easy to pretend that she is traveling alone, that she is on a journey by herself and can do as her fancy dictates. Ingrid, who traveled a lot and was versed in shipboard proprieties, kept introducing her to people she met and befriended and taught her how to behave: told her what's expected and acceptable. The girl was pleased, but was shy and preferred to be by herself. She explored the ship to her heart's content: she sat and watched the movies, she wrote to her friends, or spent time reading at a corner table in the large, spacious arena that was the library and writing room, she sat in one or another of the comfortable chairs on deck thinking and dreaming, imagining herself in some invented form of future life, as someone's fiancée, wife or mother. It was easy to imagine — simply to insert herself in the place of the young women (with husbands, children or lovers) she saw around her and to assume their different, mysterious lives.

She loved to walk on deck, close to the railing, whence she could look out on the sea. The weather was good: there was neither rain nor storm. The sea was relatively calm, but there was no sunshine: the expanse of water before her was grey; she saw nothing but water and clouds wherever she looked; it was intimidating.

"Hello, can I walk with you?" She turned around: the voice came from behind her and it belonged to a young man — very young, probably no more than twenty. He was of middle height, with dark wavy hair fashionably cut, and an open, friendly face. His eyes were warm, inviting.

"I am Marcus" he continued, "an acquaintance of Jules Grey, the friend of Ms. Ingrid. If you have no objection, we could walk together. Yes?"

He spoke in English and the girl barely understood, could barely make out what he was saying. She knew he was waiting for an answer: some sign that she approved and she caught herself giving it in spite of herself:

"I am Anny" she said, an involuntary smile on her lips as she moved to the left, making room for him by her side. Ingrid has not been idle, she reflected, lining up beaus for her.

"I have been observing you on your daily excursions, but when I look in the dining room you aren't there!"

"No, I dine with my grandfather in his room. He is a rabbi and we need special food and privacy." She blurted all this out in German, but the young man understood.

"You will have to learn English, you know! That's what they speak in America. You're lucky I understand German; I had several years of it. I don't speak it fluently, though."

"Neither do I — and I don't like to speak it, not now — not after what they did!"

It was true: she felt strange about her continued need to speak German, but it was the only way she was able to communicate with people. (She spoke no English and no French. Beside her native Yiddish, she spoke some of the Slavic languages and a little Hungarian. German had been easy for her: much of its vocabulary being familiar on account of its similarity to Yiddish. Furthermore, German and Hungarian were minority languages — and in some areas the majority spoke them — in the region where she grew up. She heard it spoken as she was growing up and was accustomed to its sound. And her mother, wary as she had been over the dangers of secular culture, somehow exempted languages from the category of forbidden subjects. She wanted her to be able to speak German: it had been one of her mother's ambitions for her as well as a source of pride when, upon instruction, the girl had acquired the rudiments of the written and spoken language).

"I can imagine" — the young man turned, looking at her inquisitively, an unspoken question on his breath.

"I don't want to talk about it!" she declared abruptly. He took the hint; they walked forward in silence.

Marcus became a frequent companion: he was friendly, solicitous and very proper. They liked to walk on deck, read in the library, listen to music, or watch a cartoon together. "Will you come to the dance tonight?" he asked innocently one morning as they emerged from their reading session. "I saw the band rehearse this morning: they sounded real good. Should be very exciting; I'm told the dances are real fun."

"I'm afraid I don't dance — I haven't been taught the steps, you see? — besides, I'm not expected to dance with boys.

"Not dance with boys? Hmm...who are you expected to dance with then? not girls?" he laughed, not comprehending the import of her statement.

"Don't worry, I'll teach you! The steps are real easy." I know you'll learn fast: why don't we practice now? The ballroom is empty — I'll teach you — you'll see what fun it is. He didn't wait for her reply, but took her by the hand and led her forward.

She didn't resist: she followed him expectantly not without awe at the prospect: is it really true? Is she going to have some casual fun — doing the things so long forbidden her that others engaged in routinely without much thought? How wonderful it must feel to be able to do so! And now she, too, will be part of it at last.

Her thoughts went back to her school days, when she had been full of yearning to have that kind of experience, to dance with the others, but all she was allowed to do was watch. Stand on the sidelines and watch. But not now! No, she will be there — she will be part of the merry crowd of dancers and no one will be the wiser. Oh, she will have to keep it to herself.

She won't be able to share her experience with them: the grandfather mustn't find out about it — why aggravate him? And that will be possible only if she manages to keep Nathan in the dark. He is zealously religious, and will consider it an obligation to inform the grandfather — to keep her from indulging in forbidden activity, the way he had done when he saw her put on lipstick for the first time. It shouldn't be difficult to keep her activities from him however: she doesn't expect him to come to the dance. Why, he isn't even out in the evenings when she and Marcus are walking on deck. She has no other misgivings about what she is about to do: Marcus is a shipboard friend: she realized — they both did — that when the journey is over they will not see each other again. But it is so much fun — yes, she will keep it so while it lasts.

They reached the ballroom and the young man led her to the middle of the vast polished dance floor.

"We will have to provide the music ourselves, but first we must position ourselves," he said laughing and deftly placed his hand around her waist.

"You should put your left arm on my shoulder, like this," he said, guiding her gently, "your right hand can hold on to mine. That's right! Now watch my feet! I will lead — you should have no problem following me — but pay attention to the rhythm of the 'music' as you take your steps!"

Presently he began humming the melody of one of the Straus waltzes. She knew the tune and joined in. Holding her gently in a firm embrace, he began waltzing with her around the shining floor.

It was exhilarating. Marcus was not what you would call tall, but she was so tiny that he towered over her: his dark eyes ablaze with youthful vigor, his lips parted in a dazzling smile that barred his strong white teeth. He is charming, she thought, so attractive! and obviously a good dancer with much practice. He moved gracefully around the floor, having no difficulty guiding her.

"You see? I told you there is nothing to it — and it's such fun, no?"

"Yes, it is." she agreed.

She loved the sensations the entire experience elicited.

Yes, she had suspected that it was fun — and it is. But she will have to practice: She is making wrong moves, has problems with the tempo, but she is nimble — she knows she will learn — and it's so wonderful to dance with him...

"It will be even more fun with real music!" he says.

"I can imagine. Now that you have me hooked, you better be there to dance with me! I depend on you to lead me."

"Trust me, I'll be there!"

She thanked him and made straight for her room. She had much to do to prepare, now that she had committed herself to attend the dance tonight .

"Oh, hi there!" Ingrid looked up from her book. She was in her robe, lounging on the sofa, reading. Her mother was out somewhere.

"You know, I almost regret we fixed you up with that nice young man. I saw you walking with him the other day — he is charming. But I hardly ever see you now — you're busy with him all the time — she teased, smiling.

"Don't blame me! The whole thing was your idea. And now he has asked me to come to the dance with him tonight and I promised to go. He even taught me how to do it! But —"

"Sounds good to me. What is the problem then?"

"I have nothing to wear!" I have no dancing clothes — what will I wear at a dance?"

"Don't worry! Leave it to Ingrid."

The dance had been splendid! The band played expertly, with distinction. Unpracticed as she was in these matters, the girl could appreciate good music, well performed. She had an ear for it; could carry a tune herself and she thrilled to the lovely sounds brought about by this expert musical group.

The large ornate ballroom was brilliantly lit and decorated with fresh flowers for the occasion. It was a formal affair: the men wore dark suits and a good number appeared in evening dress. The ladies wore gowns mostly — all in their best costumes, with beautifully done up hair in evening style.

The young girl appeared in a long navy blue skirt with ruffles at the hem, (an item from Ingrid's wardrobe) and a lovely white blouse trimmed with lace she had bought just before the journey (The skirt had to be shortened, but Ingrid was eager to help and did it herself). The girl looked radiant: the blue and white of her dress looked lovely against the pale blush in her cheek; her thick brown hair — swept up smoothly and held in place by a pink satin ribbon, culminated in a crown of curls that looked golden against the rest of her hair. It gave her height and she looked lovely. She danced much of the night: mostly with Marcus, but occasionally with another of the young men who asked her. Ingrid was present: the loveliest and gayest dancer on the floor, she was also the most experienced — lending the evening much of its gaiety and charm....

It was over now: and for her, for the young girl, it meant the end of this type of gaiety —that type of life. She knew there can be none of this in her future. Her future – "what is my future going to be like?" she wondered dreamily, looking out on the hurtling waves of the restless sea on this last day of their journey.

She had just said goodbye to Marcus, her companion these many days here on the ship. He had been pleasant and carefree and she was grateful for the many things he had taught her. Yes, she was glad he had been here. He had shown her a glimpse of a different life — a life new to her experience. So did Ingrid, her mother and many of the other people she had befriended. But she was leaving all of this behind: the ship, its crew, the crowded decks with its occupants from many different corners of the globe and walks of life. This endless sea...it, too, was coming to an end for her now. She was glad. And Marcus? was she glad to see their friendship end so suddenly? No, she wasn't. She liked him — she had enjoyed his friendship: she merely accepted the fact that he was part and parcel of the life here on this ship from all of which she will now be parting without much regret.

She was used to it. This had been her life for the last few years: no sooner had she befriended someone — some other persons who had made her isolation, her unhappiness, more bearable — than it was time to move on; time to say goodbye. It was nothing new...

She was glad to leave behind Europe, the place that held so much sorrow for her and her loved ones. Her parents, her siblings, her entire family are gone...not one of them returned... She knows they are dead, but there is no gravesite she can go to; nowhere she can point to and say: here in this spot repose my beloved parents and siblings. No! She has no such place where she might plant a flower, place a stone, or shed a tear at some definite spot and say: "Here they are, resting in peace." No!

To be able to do so would bring closure and healing: it would put to rest finally the agony; the unresolved riddle of their absence. Yes, she is familiar with, has often listened to the tale about the fate that befell the six million, but she wasn't there: she saw none of it happen and often indulges the fantasy that maybe someone — a brother... her little sister, Cousin Tova, Uncle Simon, will unexpectedly appear....

Much later it will be brought home to her that none of this is possible, at least as far as her parents and siblings are concerned. She will meet a school friend of hers on a visit to Israel who will furnish her with the exact date on which her mother and all of her siblings had died and the gruesome manner in which they did so. Her friend obtained that information from the only person, a woman, who escaped from there before the executions were carried out.

It was on a day in October of 1942. The gas chambers in the various camps had not yet been completed but executions were nevertheless underway: The entire group that had been waiting in the village of Rajovice (whence her mother had written to her) had been placed into moving trucks. Poisonous gas had been pumped into these vans as they were moving and all of the passengers gassed. After they were dead their corpses were buried, some still alive, in giant pits dug for that purpose. It was all part of celebrations the perpetrators had arranged to entertain themselves and their guests.

But the girl knew nothing of these gruesome details as she stood here and looked at the sea before her. She looked up and allowed her gaze to wander far out toward the unseen horizon she knew was lurking in the distance beyond the deep gray clouds. Tomorrow they will see the end...something new beyond the vast gray sea: a first glimpse of the landscape to become part of her yet invisible shapeless new life; that life for which she was now unconsciously reaching with wonder and hope in her heart.

AFTERWORD

This book, a coming of age story in the shadow of the Holocaust, is written in the style of a novel. It begins in the middle of events and proceeds without an historical framework. I provide here a few notes to orient the reader.

The story begins in the town of Vranov nad Topľou, Slovakia, in March 1942. The Slovak state (now the Slovak Republic) had been part of the First Czechoslovak Republic (CSR), 1918-1939. Its Jews, along with all other minorities, were treated as equals before the law in that democratic state. But that benevolent democracy, betrayed by its Allies and destroyed by Nazi Germany, no longer existed. At the beginning of the events described in this narrative, Slovakia, since 1939, had been a Fascist state organized by Hlinka, a Catholic priest, and his fellow Slovak fascists. Slovakia was presided over by Tiso, another Catholic priest (executed after the war for his crimes) and allied with the Axis powers, Slovakia executed all of the German legislation against its Jews with great speed. By December, 1942, Slovakia had deported 95% of its Jews to the German killing centers.

The other town I ran to initially was Bardejov, a resort area in Slovakia. The state I was in between August 1942 and March 1944 was Hungary. The first town in Hungary in which we stopped was Košice. That city was part of the former CSR, but was awarded to Hungary by the Nazis as part of a reward for Hungary's alliance with them, The "metropolis" referred to was the city of Budapest in Hungary.

In March, 1944, the Germans marched into Hungary. The refugees who could dispersed. I went to the city of Nitra, Slovakia. My grandparents went to Bratislava (the capital of Slovakia) referred to in this story as the City or capital City. I joined them there in September, 1944. Bratislava was my final place of residence as an illegal Jewish refugee before our trip to Switzerland, and from there, after the war, to the United States.

In 1951, I married Israel Rubin, a Judaic scholar with vast knowledge in Jewish tradition and heritage. He also pursued secular knowledge and became a sociologist. I continued my education in the United States as well, obtaining a Ph.D. in history in 1982. Despite the adolescent attractions described herein, my husband and I chose an Orthodox Jewish life and raised our children in this tradition.

Made in the USA
San Bernardino, CA
23 January 2020

63293387R00133